Lucy B.

These I Have Loved

These I Have Loved

A TREASURY OF IMMORTAL POEMS

Selected by

GILBERT HAY

AN ESSANDESS SPECIAL EDITION
NEW YORK

THESE I HAVE LOVED
A Treasury of Immortal Poems

SBN: 671–10351–2

Library of Congress Catalog Card Number: 74–99945

PRINTED IN THE U.S.A.

For Ed and Teresa Wren
great lovers

Contents

Preface

What's a poem for? To give us words for the music in ourselves. To give us words to live by; great, swinging words for our dreams to march to. Just as it takes a child to remind us of the pleasure of simple things, so it takes a poet to show us the wonders that are before our eyes.

There is power in poetry. Power to help us through difficult days. Power to relieve tension and calm the mind. There is joy in poetry. Joy that lifts the heart and makes the spirit soar.

In these days of stress and tension, rush and worry, and ever greater speed, we need poetry to remind us that there is more to life than speed and striving; that there is beauty in the world, beauty to be had in exchange for a few minutes of time.

These I Have Loved was compiled from the poetry reading of a lifetime. I hope the selections will bring you a little of the joy they have given me and those I have taught.

Love

ANONYMOUS

I love you,
Not only for what you are,
But for what I am
When I am with you.

I love you,
Not only for what
You have made of yourself,
But for what
You are making of me.

I love you
For the part of me
That you bring out;
I love you
For putting your hand
Into my heaped-up heart
And passing over
All the foolish, weak things
That you can't help
Dimly seeing there,
And for drawing out
Into the light
All the beautiful belongings
That no one else had looked
Quite far enough to find.

I love you because you
Are helping me to make
Of the lumber of my life
Not a tavern
But a temple;

Out of the works
Of my every day
Not a reproach
But a song.

The Salutation of the Dawn

ANONYMOUS

Listen to the Exhortation of the Dawn!
Look to this Day!
For it is Life, the very Life of Life.
In its brief course lie all the
Verities and Realities of your Existence:
The Bliss of Growth,
The Glory of Action,
The Splendor of Beauty,
For Yesterday is but a Dream,
And To-morrow is only a Vision:
But To-day well-lived makes
Every Yesterday a Dream of Happiness,
And every To-morrow a Vision of Hope.
Look well therefore to this Day!
Such is the Salutation of the Dawn!

BASED ON THE SANSKRIT

Dover Beach

MATTHEW ARNOLD

The sea is calm tonight.
The tide is full, the moon lies fair
Upon the straits;—on the French coast the light
Gleams and is gone; the cliffs of England stand,

Glimmering and vast, out in the tranquil bay.
Come to the window, sweet is the night-air!

Only, from the long line of spray
Where the sea meets the moon-blanched land,
Listen! you hear the grating roar
Of pebbles which the waves draw back, and fling,
At their return, up the high strand,
Begin, and cease, and then again begin,
With tremulous cadence slow, and bring
The eternal note of sadness in.

Sophocles long ago
Heard it on the Ægean, and it brought
Into his mind the turbid ebb and flow
Of human misery; we
Find also in the sound a thought,
Hearing it by this distant northern sea.

The sea of faith
Was once, too, at the full, and round earth's shore
Lay like the folds of a bright girdle furled.
But now I only hear
Its melancholy, long, withdrawing roar,
Retreating, to the breath
Of the night-wind, down the vast edges drear
And naked shingles of the world.

Ah, love, let us be true
To one another! for the world, which seems
To lie before us like a land of dreams,
So various, so beautiful, so new,
Hath really neither joy, nor love, nor light,
Nor certitude, nor peace, nor help for pain;
And we are here as on a darkling plain
Swept with confused alarms of struggle and flight,
Where ignorant armies clash by night.

America the Beautiful

KATHERINE LEE BATES

O beautiful for spacious skies,
   For amber waves of grain,
For purple mountain majesties
   Above the fruited plain!
     America! America!
   God shed His grace on thee
And crown thy good with brotherhood
   From sea to shining sea!

O beautiful for pilgrim feet,
   Whose stern, impassioned stress
A thoroughfare for freedom beat
   Across the wilderness!
     America! America!
   God mend thine every flaw,
Confirm thy soul in self-control,
   Thy liberty in law!

O beautiful for heroes proved
   In liberating strife,
Who more than self their country loved,
   And mercy more than life!
     America! America!
   May God thy gold refine
Till all success be nobleness
   And every gain divine!

O beautiful for patriot dream
   That sees beyond the years
Thine alabaster cities gleam
   Undimmed by human tears!

America! America!
God shed His grace on thee
And crown thy good with brotherhood
From sea to shining sea!

The Death and Last Confession of Wandering Peter

HILAIRE BELLOC

When Peter Wanderwide was young
He wandered everywhere he would:
And all that he approved was sung,
And most of what he saw was good.

When Peter Wanderwide was thrown
By Death himself beyond Auxerre,
He chanted in heroic tone
To priests and people gathered there:

"If all that I have loved and seen
Be with me on the Judgment Day,
I shall be saved the crowd between
From Satan and his foul array.

"Almighty God will surely cry,
'St. Michael! Who is this that stands
With Ireland in his dubious eye,
And Perigord between his hands,

"'And on his arm the stirrup-thongs,
And in his gait the narrow seas,
And in his mouth Burgundian songs,
But in his heart the Pyrenees?'

"St. Michael then will answer right
   (And not without angelic shame),
'I seem to know his face by sight:
   I cannot recollect his name . . . ?'

"St. Peter will befriend me then,
   Because my name is Peter too:
'I know him for the best of men
   That ever wallopped barley brew.

" 'And though I did not know him well
   And though his soul were clogged with sin,
I hold the keys of Heaven and Hell.
   Be welcome, noble Peterkin.'

"Then shall I spread my native wings
   And tread secure the heavenly floor,
And tell the Blessed doubtful things
   Of Val d'Aran and Perigord."

This was the last and solemn jest
   Of weary Peter Wanderwide.
He spoke it with a failing zest,
   And having spoken it, he died.

The Lamb

WILLIAM BLAKE

Little Lamb, who made thee?
Dost thou know who made thee,
Gave thee life, and bid thee feed
By the stream and o'er the mead;
Gave thee clothing of delight,

Softest clothing, woolly, bright;
Gave thee such a tender voice
Making all the vales rejoice?
   Little Lamb, who made thee?
   Dost though know who made thee?

Little Lamb, I'll tell thee,
Little Lamb, I'll tell thee;
He is called by thy name,
For He calls Himself a Lamb
He is meek, and He is mild;
He became a little child.
I a child, and thou a lamb,
We are called by His name.
   Little Lamb, God bless thee!
   Little Lamb, God bless thee.

The Tiger

WILLIAM BLAKE

Tiger! Tiger! burning bright,
In the forests of the night,
What immortal hand or eye
Could frame thy fearful symmetry?

In what distant deeps or skies
Burnt the fire of thine eyes?
On what wings dare he aspire?
What the hand dare seize the fire?

And what shoulder, and what art,
Could twist the sinews of thy heart?

And when thy heart began to beat,
What dread hand and what dread feet?

What the hammer? what the chain?
In what furnace was thy brain?
What the anvil? what dread grasp
Dare its deadly terrors clasp?

When the stars threw down their spears,
And watered heaven with their tears,
Did He smile His work to see?
Did He who made the Lamb, make thee?

Tiger! Tiger! burning bright,
In the forests of the night,
What immortal hand or eye
Dare frame thy fearful symmetry?

The Great Lover

RUPERT BROOKE

I have been so great a lover: filled my days
So proudly with the splendour of Love's praise,
The pain, the calm, and the astonishment,
Desire illimitable, and still content.
And all dear names men use, to cheat despair,
For the perplexed and viewless streams that bear
Our hearts at random down the dark of life.
Now, ere the unthinking silence on that strife
Steals down, I would cheat drowsy Death so far,
My night shall be remembered for a star
That outshone all the suns of all men's days.
Shall I not crown them with immortal praise

Whom I have loved, who have given me, dared with me
High secrets, and in darkness knelt to see
The inenarrable godhead of delight?
Love is a flame;—we have beaconed the world's night.
A city:—and we have built it, these and I.
An emperor:—we have taught the world to die.
So, for their sakes I loved, ere I go hence,
And the high cause of Love's magnificence,
And to keep loyalties young, I'll write those names
Golden for ever, eagles, crying flames,
And set them as a banner, that men may know,
To dare the generations, burn, and blow
Out on the wind of Time, shining and streaming. . . .

These I have loved:
        White plates and cups, clean-gleaming,
Ringed with blue lines; and feathery, faery dust;
Wet roofs, beneath the lamp-light; the strong crust
Of friendly bread; and many-tasting food;
Rainbows; and the blue bitter smoke of wood;
And radiant raindrops couching in cool flowers;
And flowers themselves, that sway through sunny hours,
Dreaming of moths that drink them under the moon;
Then, the cool kindliness of sheets, that soon
Smooth away trouble; and the rough male kiss
Of blankets; grainy wood; live hair that is
Shining and free; blue-massing clouds; the keen
Unpassioned beauty of a great machine;
The benison of hot water; furs to touch;
The good smell of old clothes; and other such—
The comfortable smell of friendly fingers,
Hair's fragrance, and the musty reek that lingers
About dead leaves and last year's ferns. . . .
                                Dear names,
And thousand others throng to me! Royal flames;

Sweet water's dimpling laugh from tap or spring;
Holes in the ground; and voices that do sing:
Voices in laughter, too; and body's pain,
Soon turned to peace; and the deep-panting train;
Firm sands; the little dulling edge of foam
That browns and dwindles as the wave goes home;
And washen stones, gay for an hour; the cold
Graveness of iron; moist black earthen mould;
Sleep; and high places; footprints in the dew;
And oaks; and brown horse-chestnuts, glossy-new;
And new-peeled sticks; and shining pools on grass;—
All these have been my loves. And these shall pass.
Whatever passes not, in the great hour,
Nor all my passion, all my prayers, have power
To hold them with me through the gate of Death.
They'll play deserter, turn with the traitor breath,
Break the high bond we made, and sell Love's trust
And sacramental covenant to the dust.

—Oh, never a doubt but, somewhere, I shall wake,
And give what's left of love again, and make
New friends now strangers. . . .
                              But the best I've known
Stays here, and changes, breaks, grows old, is blown
About the winds of the world, and fades from brains
Of living men, and dies.
                              Nothing remains.

O dear my loves, O faithless, once again
This one last gift I give: that after men
Shall know, and later lovers, far-removed
Praise you, "All these were lovely"; say, "He loved."

How Do I Love Thee?

ELIZABETH BARRETT BROWNING

How do I love thee? Let me count the ways.
I love thee to the depth and breadth and height
My soul can reach, when feeling out of sight
For the ends of Being and ideal Grace.
I love thee to the level of every day's
Most quiet need, by sun and candlelight.
I love thee freely, as men strive for Right;
I love thee purely, as they turn from Praise.
I love thee with the passion put to use
In my old griefs, and with my childhood's faith.
I love thee with a love I seemed to lose
With my lost saints,—I love thee with the breath,
Smiles, tears, of all my life!—and, if God choose,
I shall but love thee better after death.

Summum Bonum

ROBERT BROWNING

All the breath and the bloom of the year
in the bag of one bee;
    All the wonder and wealth of the mine
in the heart of one gem;
In the core of one pearl all the shade and
the shine of the sea;
    Breath and bloom, shade and shine,—
wonder, wealth, and—how far above them—
        Truth, that's brighter than gem,
        Truth, that's purer than pearl,—
Brightest truth, purest trust in the universe—
all were for me
        In the kiss of one girl.

Prospice

ROBERT BROWNING

Fear death?—to feel the fog in my throat,
  The mist in my face,
When the snows begin, and the blasts denote
  I am nearing the place,
The power of the night, the press of the storm,
  The post of the foe;
Where he stands, the Arch Fear in a visible form,
  Yet the strong man must go:
For the journey is done and the summit attained,
  And the barriers fall,
Though a battle's to fight ere the guerdon be gained,
  The reward of it all.
I was ever a fighter, so—one fight more,
  The best and the last!
I would hate that death bandaged my eyes, and forbore,
  And bade me creep past.
No! let me taste the whole of it, fare like my peers
  The heroes of old,
Bear the brunt, in a minute pay glad life's arrears
  Of pain, darkness and cold.
For sudden the worst turns the best to the brave,
  The black minute's at end,
And the elements' rage, the fiend-voices that rave,
  Shall dwindle, shall blend,
Shall change, shall become first a peace out of pain,
  Then a light, then thy breast,
O thou soul of my soul! I shall clasp thee again,
  And with God be the rest!

Thanatopsis

WILLIAM CULLEN BRYANT

To him who in the love of nature holds
Communion with her visible forms, she speaks
A various language; for his gayer hours
She has a voice of gladness, and a smile
And eloquence of beauty, and she glides
Into his darker musings, with a mild
And healing sympathy, that steals away
Their sharpness, ere he is aware. When thoughts
Of the last bitter hour come like a blight
Over thy spirit, and sad images
Of the stern agony, and shroud, and pall,
And breathless darkness, and the narrow house,
Make thee to shudder and grow sick at heart;—
Go forth, under the open sky, and list
To Nature's teachings, while from all around—
Earth and her waters, and the depths of air—
Comes a still voice:
     Yet a few days, and thee
The all-beholding sun shall see no more
In all his course; nor yet in the cold ground,
Where thy pale form was laid, with many tears,
Nor in the embrace of ocean, shall exist
Thy image. Earth, that nourished thee, shall claim
Thy growth, to be resolved to earth again,
And, lost each human trace, surrendering up
Thine individual being, shalt thou go
To mix forever with the elements,
To be a brother to the insensible rock
And to the sluggish clod, which the rude swain
Turns with his share, and treads upon. The oak
Shall send his roots abroad, and pierce thy mold.

Yet not to thine eternal resting-place
Shalt thou retire alone, nor couldst thou wish
Couch more magnificent. Thou shalt lie down
With patriarchs of the infant world—with kings,
The powerful of the earth—the wise, the good,
Fair forms, and hoary seers of ages past,
All in one mighty sepulchre. The hills
Rock-ribbed and ancient as the sun,—the vales
Stretching in pensive quietness between;
The venerable woods—rivers that move
In majesty, and the complaining brooks
That make the meadows green; and, poured round all,
Old Ocean's gray and melancholy waste,—
Are but the solemn decorations all
Of the great tomb of man. The golden sun,
The planets, all the infinite host of heaven,
Are shining on the sad abodes of death
Through the still lapse of ages. All that tread
The globe are but a handful to the tribes
That slumber in its bosom.—Take the wings
Of morning, pierce the Barcan wilderness,
Or lose thyself in the continuous woods
Where rolls the Oregon, and hears no sound,
Save his own dashings—yet the dead are there:
And millions in those solitudes, since first
The flight of years began, have laid them down
In their last sleep—the dead reign there alone.

So shalt thou rest, and what if thou withdraw
In silence from the living, and no friend
Take note of thy departure? All that breathe
Will share thy destiny. The gay will laugh
When thou art gone, the solemn brood of care
Plod on, and each one as before will chase
His favorite phantom; yet all these shall leave
Their mirth and their employments, and shall come
And make their bed with thee. As the long train

Of ages glides away, the sons of men—
The youth in life's fresh spring, and he who goes
In the full strength of years, matron and maid,
The speechless babe, and the gray-headed man—
Shall one by one be gathered to thy side,
By those, who in their turn shall follow them.

So live, that when thy summons comes to join
The innumerable caravan, which moves
To that mysterious realm, where each shall take
His chamber in the silent halls of death,
Thou go not, like the quarry-slave at night,
Scourged to his dungeon, but, sustained and soothed
By an unfaltering trust, approach thy grave
Like one who wraps the drapery of his couch
About him, and lies down to pleasant dreams.

To a Mouse

ROBERT BURNS

Wee, sleekit, cow'rin', tim'rous beastie,
O, what a panic's in thy breastie!
Thou need na start awa' sae hasty,
   Wi' bickering brattle!
I wad be laith to rin an' chase thee,
   Wi' murd'ring pattle!

I'm truly sorry man's dominion
Has broken Nature's social union,
An' justifies that ill opinion,
Which makes thee startle
At me, thy poor, earth-born companion,
An' fellow-mortal!

I doubt na, whiles, but thou may thieve;
What then? poor beastie, thou maun live!
A daimen icker in a thrave
    'S a sma' request:
I'll get a blessin' wi' the lave,
    And never miss 't!

Thy wee bit housie, too, in ruin!
Its silly wa's the win's are strewin'!
An' naething, now, to big a new ane,
    O' foggage green!
An' bleak December's winds ensuin',
    Baith snell an' keen!

Thou saw the fields laid bare an' waste,
An' weary winter comin' fast,
An' cozie here, beneath the blast,
    Thou thought to dwell,—
Till, crash! the cruel coulter passed
    Out through thy cell.

That wee bit heap o' leaves an' stibble
Has cost thee mony a weary nibble!
Now thou's turned out, for a' thy trouble,
    But house or hald,
To thole the winter's sleety dribble,
    An' cranreuch cauld!

But, Mousie, thou art no thy lane,
In proving foresight may be vain:
The best-laid schemes o' mice an' men,
    Gang aft a-gley,
An' lea'e us nought but grief an' pain,
    For promised joy!

Still thou art blest, compared wi' me!
The present only toucheth thee:
But, Och! I backward cast my e'e
   On prospects drear!
An' forward, though I canna see,
   I guess an' fear!

The Destruction of Sennacherib

GEORGE GORDON BYRON

The Assyrian came down like the wolf on the fold,
And his cohorts were gleaming in purple and gold;
And the sheen of their spears was like stars on the sea,
When the blue wave rolls nightly on deep Galilee.

Like the leaves of the forest when Summer is green,
That host with their banners at sunset were seen:
Like the leaves of the forest when Autumn hath blown,
That host on the morrow lay withered and strown.

For the Angel of Death spread his wings on the blast,
And breathed in the face of the foe as he passed;
And the eyes of the sleepers waxed deadly and chill,
And their hearts but once heaved, and for ever grew still!

And there lay the steed with his nostril all wide,
But through it there rolled not the breath of his pride:
And the foam of his gasping lay white on the turf,
And cold as the spray of the rock-beating surf.

And there lay the rider distorted and pale,
With the dew on his brow, and the rust on his mail;
And the tents were all silent, the banners alone,
The lances unlifted, the trumpet unblown.

And the widows of Ashur are loud in their wail,
And the idols are broke in the temple of Baal;
And the might of the Gentile, unsmote by the sword,
Hath melted like snow in the glance of the Lord!

Lepanto

GILBERT KEITH CHESTERTON

White founts falling in the courts of the sun,
And the Soldan of Byzantium is smiling as they run;
There is laughter like the fountains in that face of all men
    feared,
It stirs the forest darkness, the darkness of his beard;
It curls the blood-red crescent, the crescent of his lips;
For the inmost sea of all the earth is shaken with his ships.
They have dared the white republics up the capes of Italy,
They have dashed the Adriatic round the Lion of the Sea,
And the Pope has cast his arms abroad for agony and loss,
And called the kings of Christendom for swords about the
    Cross.
The cold queen of England is looking in the glass;
The shadow of the Valois is yawning at the Mass;
From evening isles fantastical rings faint the Spanish gun,
And the Lord upon the Golden Horn is laughing in the
    sun.

Dim drums throbbing, in the hills half heard,
Where only on a nameless throne a crownless prince has
    stirred,
Where, risen from a doubtful seat and half-attainted stall,
The last knight of Europe takes weapons from the wall,
The last and lingering troubadour to whom the bird has
    sung,
That once went singing southward when all the world was
    young.

In that enormous silence, tiny and unafraid;
Comes up along a winding road the noise of the Crusade.

Strong gongs groaning as the guns boom far,
Don John of Austria is going to the war;
Stiff flags straining in the night-blasts cold
In the gloom black-purple, in the glint old-gold,
Torchlight crimson on the copper kettle-drums,
Then the tuckets, then the trumpets, then the cannon, and
    he comes.
Don John laughing in the brave beard curled,
Spurning of his stirrups like the thrones of all the world,
Holding his head up for a flag of all the free.
Love-light of Spain—hurrah!
Death-light of Africa!
Don John of Austria
Is riding to the sea.

Mahound is in his paradise above the evening star,
(*Don John of Austria is going to the war.*)
He moves a mighty turban on the timeless houri's knees,
His turban that is woven of the sunset and the seas.
He shakes the peacock gardens as he rises from his ease,
And he strides among the tree-tops and it taller than the
    trees;
And his voice through all the garden is a thunder sent to
    bring
Black Azrael and Ariel and Ammon on the wing.
Giants and the Genii,
Multiplex of wing and eye,
Whose strong obedience broke the sky
When Solomon was king.

They rush in red and purple from the red clouds of the
    morn,
From temples where the yellow gods shut up their eyes in
    scorn;

They rise in green robes roaring from the green hells of
    the sea
Where fallen skies and evil hues and eyeless creatures be,
On them the sea-valves cluster and the grey sea-forests
    curl,
Splashed with a splendid sickness, the sickness of the
    pearl;
They swell in sapphire smoke out of the blue cracks of the
    ground,—
They gather and they wonder and give worship to
    Mahound.
And he saith, "Break up the mountains where the hermit-
    folk may hide,
And sift the red and silver sands lest bone of saint abide,
And chase the Giaours flying night and day, not giving
    rest,
For that which was our trouble comes again out of the
    west
We have set the seal of Solomon on all things under sun,
Of knowledge and of sorrow and endurance of things
    done.
But a noise is in the mountains, in the mountains, and
    I know
The voice that shook our palaces—four hundred years
    ago:
It is he that saith not 'Kismet': it is he that knows not
    Fate;
It is Richard, it is Raymond, it is Godfrey in the gate!
It is he whose loss is laughter when he counts the wager
    worth,
Put down your feet upon him, that our peace be on the
    earth."
For he heard drums groaning and he heard guns jar,
(*Don John of Austria is going to the war.*)
Sudden and still—hurrah!

Bolt from Iberia!
Don John of Austria
Is gone by Alcalar.

St. Michael's on his Mountain in the sea-roads of the north
(*Don John of Austria is girt and going forth.*)
Where the grey seas glitter and the sharp tides shift
And the sea folk labour and the red sails lift.
He shakes his lance of iron and he claps his wings of stone;
The noise is gone through Normandy; the noise is gone
    alone;
The North is full of tangled things and texts and aching
    eyes
And dead is all the innocence of anger and surprise,
And Christian killeth Christian in a narrow dusty room,
And Christian dreadeth Christ that hath a newer face of
    doom,
And Christian hateth Mary that God kissed in Galilee,—
But Don John of Austria is riding to the sea.
Don John calling through the blast and the eclipse,
Crying with the trumpet, with the trumpet of his lips,
Trumpet that sayeth ha!
    Domino gloria!
Don John of Austria
Is shouting to the ships.

King Philip's in his closet with the Fleece about his neck
(*Don John of Austria is armed upon the deck.*)
The walls are hung with velvet that is black and soft as
    sin,
And little dwarfs creep out of it and little dwarfs creep in.
He holds a crystal phial that has colours like the moon,
He touches, and it tingles, and he trembles very soon,
And his face is as a fungus of a leprous white and gray
Like plants in the high houses that are shuttered from the
    day,

And death is in the phial, and the end of noble work,
But Don John of Austria has fired upon the Turk.
Don John's hunting, and his hounds have bayed—
Booms away past Italy the rumor of his raid.
Gun upon gun, ha! ha!
Gun upon gun, hurrah!
Don John of Austria
Has loosed the cannonade.

The Pope was in his chapel before day or battle broke,
(*Don John of Austria is hidden in the smoke.*)
The hidden room in a man's house where God sits all the
    year,
The secret window whence the world looks small and very
    dear.
He sees as in a mirror on the monstrous twilight sea
The cresent of his cruel ships whose name is mystery;
They fling great shadows foe-wards, making Cross and
    Castle dark,
They veil the plumèd lions on the galleys of St. Mark;
And above the ships are palaces of brown, black-bearded
    chiefs,
And below the ship are prisons, where with multitudinous
    griefs,
Christian captives sick and sunless, all a labouring race
    repines
Like a race in sunken cities, like a nation in the mines.
They are lost like slaves that swat, and in the skies of
    morning hung
The stairways of the tallest gods when tyranny was young.
They are countless, voiceless, hopeless as those fallen or
    fleeing on
Before the high Kings' horses in the granite of Babylon.
And many a one grows witless in his quiet room in hell
Where a yellow face looks inward through the lattice of
    his cell,

And he finds his God forgotten, and he seeks no more a
  sign—
(*But Don John of Austria has burst the battle-line!*)
Don John pounding from the slaughter-painted poop,
Purpling all the ocean like a bloody pirate's sloop,
Scarlet running over on the silvers and the golds,
Breaking of the hatches up and bursting of the holds,
Thronging of the thousands up that labour under sea
White for bliss and blind for sun and stunned for liberty.
Vivat Hispania!
Domino Gloria!
Don John of Austria
Has set his people free!

Cervantes on his galley sets the sword back in the sheath
(*Don John of Austria rides homeward with a wreath.*)
And he sees across a weary land a staggling road in Spain,
Up which a lean and foolish knight forever rides in vain,
And he smiles, but not as Sultans smile, and settles back
  the blade. . . .
(*But Don John of Austria rides home from the Crusade.*)

Thirty Bob a Week

JOHN DAVIDSON

I couldn't touch a step and turn a screw,
  And set the blooming world a-work for me,
Like such as cut their teeth—I hope, like you—
  On the handle of a skeleton gold key;
I cut mine on a leek, which I eat it every week:
  I'm a clerk at thirty bob as you can see.

But I don't allow it's luck and all a toss;
  There's no such thing as being starred and crossed;
It's just the power of some to be a boss,
  And the bally power of others to be bossed:
I face the music, sir; you bet I ain't a cur;
  Strike me lucky if I don't believe I'm lost!

For like a mole I journey in the dark,
  A-travelling along the underground
From my Pillar'd Halls and broad Suburban Park,
  To come the daily dull official round;
And home again at night with my pipe all alight,
  A-scheming how to count ten bob a pound.

And it's often very cold and very wet,
  And my missis stitches towels for a hunks;
And the Pillar'd Halls is half of it to let—
  Three rooms about the size of travelling trunks.
And we cough, my wife and I, to dislocate a sigh,
  When the noisy little kids are in their bunks.

But you never hear her do a growl or whine,
  For she's made of flint and roses, very odd;
And I've got to cut my meaning rather fine,
  Or I'd blubber, for I'm made of greens and sod:
So p'r'aps we are in Hell for all that I can tell,
  And lost and damn'd and served up hot to God.

I ain't blaspheming, Mr. Silver-tongue;
  I'm saying things a bit beyond your art:
Of all the rummy starts you ever sprung,
  Thirty bob a week's the rummiest start!
With your science and your books and your the'ries about
    spooks,
  Did you ever hear of looking in your heart?

I didn't mean your pocket, Mr., no:
    I mean that having children and a wife,
With thirty bob on which to come and go,
    Isn't dancing to the tabor and fife:
When it doesn't make you drink, by Heaven! it makes you
      think,
    And notice curious items about life.

I step into my heart and there I meet
    A god-almighty devil singing small,
Who would like to shout and whistle in the street,
    And squelch the passers flat against the wall;
If the whole world was a cake he had the power to take,
    He would take it, ask for more, and eat it all.

And I meet a sort of simpleton beside,
    The kind that life is always giving beans;
With thirty bob a week to keep a bride
    He fell in love and married in his teens:
At thirty bob he stuck; but he knows it isn't luck:
    He knows the seas are deeper than tureens.

And the god-almighty devil and the fool
    That meet me in the High Street on the strike,
When I walk about my heart a-gathering wool,
    Are my good and evil angels if you like.
And both of them together in every kind of weather
    Ride me like a double-seated bike.

That's rough a bit and needs its meaning curled.
    But I have a high old hot un in my mind—
A most engrugious notion of the world,
    That leaves your lightning 'rithmetic behind:
I give it at a glance when I say "There ain't no chance,
    Nor nothing of the lucky-lottery kind."

And it's this way I make it out to be:
　　No fathers, mothers, countries, climates—none;
Not Adam was responsible for me,
　　Nor society, nor systems, nary one:
A little sleeping seed, I woke—I did, indeed—
　　A million years before the blooming sun.

I woke because I thought the time had come;
　　Beyond my will there was no other cause;
And every where I found myself at home,
　　Because I chose to be the thing I was;
And in what ever shape of mollusc or of ape
　　I always went according to the laws.

I was the love that chose my mother out;
　　I joined two lives and from the union burst;
My weakness and my strength without a doubt
　　Are mine alone for ever from the first:
It's just the very same with a difference in the name
　　As "Thy will be done." You say it if you durst!

They say it daily up and down the land
　　As easy as you take a drink, it's true;
But the difficultest go to understand,
　　And the difficultest job a man can do,
Is to come it brave and meek with thirty bob a week,
　　And feel that that's the proper thing for you.

It's a naked child against a hungry wolf;
　　It's playing bowls upon a splitting wreck;
It's walking on a string across a gulf
　　With millstones fore-and-aft about your neck;
But the thing is daily done by many and many a one;
　　And we fall, face forward, fighting, on the deck.

Leisure

W. H. DAVIES

What is this life if, full of care,
We have no time to stand and stare.

No time to stand beneath the boughs
And stare as long as sheep or cows.

No time to see, when woods we pass,
Where squirrels hide their nuts in grass.

No time to see in broad daylight,
Streams full of stars, like skies at night.

No time to turn at Beauty's glance,
And watch her feet, how they can dance.

No time to wait till her mouth can
Enrich that smile her eyes began.

A poor life this if, full of care,
We have no time to stand and stare.

If I Can Stop One Heart from Breaking

EMILY DICKINSON

If I can stop one heart from breaking
I shall not live in vain
If I can ease one life the aching
Or cool one pain
Or help one fainting robin
Unto his nest again
I shall not live in vain.

I Never Saw a Moor

EMILY DICKINSON

I never saw a Moor—
I never saw the Sea—
Yet know I how the Heather looks
And what a wave must be.

I never spoke with God
Nor visited in Heaven—
Yet certain am I of the spot
As if the chart were given.

My Life Closed Twice

EMILY DICKINSON

My life closed twice before its close—
It yet remains to see
If Immortality unveil
A third event to me.

So huge, so hopeless to conceive
As these that twice befell.
Parting is all we know of heaven,
And all we need of hell.

In After Days

AUSTIN DOBSON

In after days when grasses high
O'er-top the stone where I shall lie,
    Though ill or well the world adjust
    My slender claim to honored dust,
I shall not question or reply.

I shall not see the morning sky;
I shall not hear the night-wind sigh;
    I shall be mute, as all men must
        In after days!

But yet, now living, fain were I
That some one then should testify,
    Saying—"He held his pen in trust
    To Art, not serving shame or lust."
Will none?—Then let my memory die
        In after days!

Death, Be Not Proud

JOHN DONNE

Death, be not proud, though some have callèd thee
Mighty and dreadful, for thou art not so:
For those whom thou think'st thou dost overthrow
Die not, poor Death; nor yet canst thou kill me.
From rest and sleep, which but thy picture be,
Much pleasure; then from thee much more must flow;
And soonest our best men with thee do go—
Rest of their bones and souls' delivery!
Thou'rt slave to fate, chance, kings, and desperate men,
And dost with poison, war, and sickness dwell;
And poppy or charms can make us sleep as well
And better than thy stroke. Why swell'st thou then?
One short sleep past, we wake eternally,
And Death shall be no more: Death, thou shalt die!

Journey of the Magi

T. S. ELIOT

"A cold coming we had of it,
Just the worst time of the year
For a journey, and such a long journey:
The ways deep and the weather sharp,
The very dead of winter."
And the camels galled, sore-footed, refractory,
Lying down in the melting snow.
There were times we regretted
The summer palaces on slopes, the terraces,
And the silken girls bringing sherbet.
Then the camel men cursing and grumbling
And running away, and wanting their liquor and women
And the night-fires going out, and the lack of shelters,
And the cities hostile and the towns unfriendly
And the villages dirty and charging high prices:
A hard time we had of it.
At the end we preferred to travel all night,
Sleeping in snatches,
With the voices singing in our ears, saying
That this was all folly.

Then at dawn we came down to a temperate valley,
Wet, below the snow line, smelling of vegetation,
With a running stream and a water-mill beating the
    darkness,
And three trees on the low sky,
And an old white horse galloped away in the meadow.
Then we came to a tavern with vine-leaves over the lintel,
Six hands at an open door dicing for pieces of silver,
And feet kicking the empty wine-skins.
But there was no information, and so we continued
And arrived at evening, not a moment too soon
Finding the place; it was (you may say) satisfactory.

All this was a long time ago, I remember,
And I would do it again, but set down
This set down
This: were we led all that way for
Birth or Death? There was a Birth, certainly,
We had evidence and no doubt. I had seen birth and
     death,
But had thought they were different; this Birth was
Hard and bitter agony for us, like Death, our death.
We returned to our places, these Kingdoms,
But no longer at ease here, in the old dispensation,
With an alien people clutching their gods.
I should be glad of another death.

The Geranium

LEONARD FEENEY, S. J.

If you wish to grow a lily
    With its white and golden hue
You will have to have a mansion
    And a gardener or two.

If you fondle a chrysanthemum
    From Spring to early Fall,
It may consent to bloom a bit,
    If it ever blooms at all.

A rose must have a radiant bush
    With lots of room and air;
And a peony wants the terrace
    Of a multimillionaire;

But all a poor geranium
    Will ever ask a man—
Is a little bit of fragrant earth
    And an old tomato can.

The House by the Side of the Road

SAM WALTER FOSS

There are hermit souls that live withdrawn
    In the place of their self-content;
There are souls like stars, that dwell apart,
    In a fellowless firmament;
There are pioneer souls that blaze their paths
    Where highways never ran—
But let me live by the side of the road
    And be a friend to man.

Let me live in a house by the side of the road
    Where the race of men go by—
The men who are good and the men who are bad,
    As good and as bad as I.
I would not sit in the scorner's seat,
    Or hurl the cynic's ban—
Let me live in a house by the side of the road
    And be a friend to man.

I see from my house by the side of the road,
    By the side of the highway of life,
The men who press with the ardor of hope,
    The men who are faint with the strife.
But I turn not away from their smiles nor their tears,
    Both parts of an infinite plan—
Let me live in my house by the side of the road
    And be a friend to man.

I know there are brook-gladdened meadows ahead,
    And mountains of wearisome height;
That the road passes on through the long afternoon
    And stretches away to the night.
But still I rejoice when the travelers rejoice
    And weep with the strangers that moan,
Nor live in a house by the side of the road
    Like a man who dwells alone.

Let me live in my house by the side of the road,
    It's here the race of men go by—
They are good, they are bad, they are weak, they are
        strong,
    Wise, foolish—so am I;
Then why should I sit in the scorner's seat,
    Or hurl the cynic's ban?
Let me live in my house by the side of the road
    And be a friend to man.

Prayer for Peace

SAINT FRANCIS OF ASSISI

Lord, make me an instrument of your peace;
Where there is hatred, let me sow love;
Where there is injury, pardon;
Where there is doubt, faith;
Where there is despair, hope;
Where there is darkness, light;
And where there is sadness, joy.

O Divine Master, grant that I may not
Seek to be consoled as to console;
To be understood as to understand;
To be loved as to love;

For it is in giving that we receive,
It is in pardoning that we are pardoned,
And it is in dying that we are born to eternal life.

The Road Not Taken

ROBERT FROST

Two roads diverged in a yellow wood,
And sorry I could not travel both
And be one traveler, long I stood
And looked down one as far as I could
To where it bent in the undergrowth;

Then took the other, as just as fair,
And having perhaps the better claim,
Because it was grassy and wanted wear;
Though as for that the passing there
Had worn them really about the same,

And both that morning equally lay
In leaves no step had trodden black.
Oh, I kept the first for another day!
Yet knowing how way leads on to way,
I doubted if I should ever come back.

I shall be telling this with a sigh
Somewhere ages and ages hence:
Two roads diverged in a wood, and I—
I took the one less traveled by,
And that has made all the difference.

Selections from Prayers from the Ark

CARMEN BERNOS DE GASZTOLD
Translated by Rumer Godden

The Prayer of the Cock

Do not forget, Lord,
it is I who make the sun rise.
I am Your servant
but, with the dignity of my calling,
I need some glitter and ostentation.
Noblesse oblige. . . .
All the same,
I am Your servant,
only . . . do not forget, Lord,
I make the sun rise.   Amen

The Prayer of the Dog

Lord,
I keep watch!
If I am not here
who will guard their house?
Watch over their sheep?
Be faithful?
No one but You and I
understands
what faithfulness is.
They call me, "Good dog! Nice dog!"
Words. . .
I take their pats
and the old bones they throw me
and I seem pleased.
They really believe they make me happy.
I take kicks too
when they come my way.
None of that matters.

I keep watch!
Lord,
do not let me die
until, for them,
all danger is driven away.   Amen

The Prayer of the Cricket

O God,
I am little and very black,
but I thank You
for having shed
Your warm sun
and the quivering of Your golden corn
on my humble life.
Then take—but be forbearing, Lord—
this little impulse of my love:
this note of music
You have set thrilling in my heart.   Amen

Elegy Written in a Country Church Yard

THOMAS GRAY

The curfew tolls the knell of parting day,
   The lowing herd winds slowly o'er the lea,
The ploughman homeward plods his weary way,
   And leaves the world to darkness and to me.

Now fades the glimmering landscape on the sight,
   And all the air a solemn stillness holds,
Save where the beetle wheels his droning flight,
   And drowsy tinklings lull the distant folds;

Save that, from yonder ivy-mantled tower,
   The moping owl does to the moon complain

Of such as, wandering near her secret bower,
    Molest her ancient, solitary reign.

Beneath those rugged elms, that yew-tree's shade,
    Where heaves the turf in many a moldering heap,
Each in his narrow cell forever laid,
    The rude forefathers of the hamlet sleep.

The breezy call of incense-breathing morn,
    The swallow twittering from the straw-built shed,
The cock's shrill clarion, or the echoing horn,
    No more shall rouse them from their lowly bed.

For them no more the blazing hearth shall burn,
    Or busy housewife ply her evening care;
No children run to lisp their sire's return,
    Or climb his knees the envied kiss to share.

Oft did the harvest to their sickle yield,
    Their furrow oft the stubborn glebe has broke;
How jocund did they drive their team afield!
    How bowed the woods beneath their sturdy stroke!

Let not ambition mock their useful toil,
    Their homely joys, and destiny obscure;
Nor grandeur hear with a disdainful smile
    The short and simple annals of the poor.

The boast of heraldry, the pomp of power,
    And all that beauty, all that wealth e'er gave
Awaits alike the inevitable hour:
    The paths of glory lead but to the grave.

Nor you, ye proud, impute to these the fault,
    If memory o'er their tomb no trophies raise
Where through the long-drawn aisle and fretted vault
    The pealing anthem swells the note of praise.

Can storied urn or animated bust
   Back to its mansion call the fleeting breath?
Can Honor's voice provoke the silent dust
   Or Flattery soothe the dull cold ear of Death?

Perhaps in this neglected spot is laid
   Some heart once pregnant with celestial fire:
Hands that the rod of empire might have swayed,
   Or wak'd to ecstasy the living lyre;

But Knowledge to their eyes her ample page,
   Rich with the spoils of time, did ne'er unroll;
Chill Penury repressed their noble rage,
   And froze the genial current of the soul.

Full many a gem of purest ray serene
   The dark, unfathomed caves of ocean bear:
Full many a flower is born to blush unseen,
   And waste its sweetness on the desert air.

Some village Hampden, that, with dauntless breast,
   The little tyrant of his fields withstood,
Some mute, inglorious Milton, here may rest;
   Some Cromwell guiltless of his country's blood.

The applause of list'ning senates to command,
   The threats of pain and ruin to despise,
To scatter plenty o'er a smiling land,
   And read their history in a nation's eyes,

Their lot forbade; nor circumscribed alone
   Their growing virtues, but their crimes confined;
Forbade to wade thro' slaughter to a throne,
   And shut the gates of mercy on mankind;

The struggling pangs of conscious truth to hide,
   To quench the blushes of ingenuous shame,

Or heap the shrine of Luxury and Pride
  With incense kindled at the Muse's flame.

Far from the madding crowd's ignoble strife,
  Their sober wishes never learned to stray;
Along the cool, sequestered vale of life
  They kept the noiseless tenor of their way.

Yet even these bones from insult to protect,
  Some frail memorial still erected nigh,
With uncouth rhymes and shapeless sculpture decked,
  Implores the passing tribute of a sigh.

Their names, their years, spelt by the unlettered Muse,
  The place of fame and elegy supply:
And many a holy text around she strews
  That teach the rustic moralist to die.

For who, to dumb forgetfulness a prey,
  This pleasing anxious being e'er resigned,
Left the warm precincts of the cheerful day,
  Nor cast one longing, lingering look behind?

On some fond breast the parting soul relies,
  Some pious drops the closing eye requires;
Ev'n from the tomb the voice of Nature cries,
  Ev'n in our ashes live their wonted fires.

For thee who, mindful of the unhonor'd dead,
  Dost in these lines their artless tale relate;
If chance, by lonely contemplation led,
  Some kindred spirit shall inquire thy fate,—

Haply some hoary-headed swain may say:
  "Oft have we seen him, at the peep of dawn,
Brushing with hasty steps the dews away,
  To meet the sun upon the upland lawn.

"There at the foot of yonder nodding beech,
    That wreathes its old fantastic roots so high,
His listless length at noontide would he stretch,
    And pore upon the brook that babbles by.

"Hard by yon wood, now smiling as in scorn,
    Mutt'ring his wayward fancies, he would rove;
Now drooping, woeful-wan, like one forlorn,
    Or craz'd with care, or cross'd in hopeless love.

"One morn I missed him on the custom'd hill,
    Along the heath, and near his favorite tree;
Another came,—nor yet beside the rill,
    Nor up the lawn, nor at the wood was he:

"The next, with dirges due, in sad array,
    Slowly through the church-way path we saw him
        borne;—
Approach and read (for thou canst read) the lay
    Grav'd on the stone beneath yon aged thorn."

THE EPITAPH

Here rest his head upon the lap of earth,
    A youth to fortune and to fame unknown;
Fair Science frown'd not on his humble birth,
    And Melancholy mark'd him for her own.

Large was his bounty, and his soul sincere;
    Heaven did a recompense as largely send:
He gave to misery all he had, a tear;
    He gained from heaven ('twas all he wished) a friend.

No farther seek his merits to disclose,
    Or draw his frailties from their dread abode,—
(There they alike in trembling hope repose),
    The bosom of his Father and his God.

Death and General Putnam

ARTHUR GUITERMAN

His iron arm had spent its force,
No longer might he rein a horse;
Lone, beside the dying blaze
Dreaming dreams of younger days
   Sat old Israel Putnam.

Twice he heard, then three times more
A knock upon the oaken door,
A knock he could not fail to know,
That old man in the ember-glow,
   "Come," said General Putnam.

The door swung wide; in cloak and hood
Lean and tall the pilgrim stood
And spoke in tones none else might hear,
"Once more I come to bring you Fear!"
   "Fear?" said General Putnam.

"You know not Fear? And yet this face
Your eyes have seen in many a place
Since first in stony Pomfret, when
You dragged the mad wolf from her den."
   "Yes," said General Putnam.

"Was I not close, when, stripped and bound
With blazing fagots heaped around
You heard the Huron war cry shrill?
Was I not close at Bunker Hill?"
   "Close," said General Putnam.

"Am I not that which strong men dread
On stricken field or fevered bed

On gloomy trail and stormy sea,
And dare you name my name to me?"
  "Death," said General Putnam.

"We have been comrades, you and I,
In chase and war beneath this sky;
And now, whatever Fate may send,
Old comrade, can you call me friend?"
  "Friend!" said General Putnam.

Then up he rose, and forth they went
Away from battleground, fortress, tent,
Mountain, wilderness, field and farm,
Death and the General, arm-in-arm,
  Death and General Putnam.

Jim Bludso of the Prairie Belle

JOHN HAY

Wall, no! I can't tell whar he lives,
  Because he don't live, you see;
Leastways, he's got out of the habit
  Of livin' like you and me.
Whar have you been for the last three year
  That you haven't heard folks tell
How Jimmy Bludso passed in his checks
  The night of the Prairie Belle?

He weren't no saint,—them engineers
  Is all pretty much alike,—
One wife in Natchez-under-the-Hill
  And another one here, in Pike;

A keerless man in his talk, was Jim,
  And an awkward hand in a row,
But he never flunked, and he never lied—
  I reckon he never knowed how.

And this was all the religion he had,—
  To treat his engine well;
Never be passed on the river;
  To mind the pilot's bell;
And if ever the Prairie Belle took fire,—
  A thousand times he swore
He'd hold her nozzle agin the bank
  Till the last soul got ashore.

All boats has their day on the Mississip,
  And her day come at last,—
The Movastar was a better boat,
  But the Belle she *wouldn't* be passed.
And so she come tearin' along that night—
  The oldest craft on the line—
With a nigger squat on her safety-valve,
  And her furnace crammed, rosin and pine.

The fire bust out as she clared the bar
  And burnt a hole in the night,
And quick as a flash she turned, and made
  For that willer-bank on the right.
There was runnin' and cursin', but Jim yelled out,
  Over all the infernal roar,
"I'll hold her nozzle agin the bank
  Till the last galoot's ashore."

Through the hot, black breath of the burnin' boat
  Jim Bludso's voice was heard,
And they all had trust in his cussedness,
  And knowed he would keep his word.

And, sure's you're born, they all got off
    Afore the smoke-stacks fell,—
And Bludso's ghost went up alone
    In the smoke of the Prairie Belle.

He weren't no saint,—but at jedgment
    I'd run my chance with Jim,
'Longside of some pious gentlemen
    That wouldn't shook hands with him.
He seen his duty, a dead-sure thing,—
    And went for it thar and then;
And Christ ain't a going to be too hard
    On a man that died for men.

A *sampling of* Grooks

PIET HEIN

Mankind

Men, said the Devil,
are good to their brothers:
they don't want to mend
their own ways but each other's.

Lest Fools Should Fail

True wisdom knows
it must comprise
some nonsense
as a compromise,
lest fools should fail
to find it wise.

The Miracle of Spring

We glibly talk
    of nature's laws,
but do things have
    a natural cause?

Black earth becoming
    yellow crocus
is undiluted
    hocus-pocus.

The Road to Wisdom

The road to wisdom?—Well, it's
plain and simple to express:
    Err
    and err
    and err again
    but less
    and less
    and less.

The Cure for Exhaustion

Sometimes, exhausted
with toil and endeavor,
I wish I could sleep
for ever and ever;
but then this reflection
my longing allays:
I shall be doing it
one of these days.

Invictus

WILLIAM ERNEST HENLEY

Out of the night that covers me,
    Black as the Pit from pole to pole,
I thank whatever gods may be
    For my unconquerable soul.

In the fell clutch of circumstance
    I have not winced nor cried aloud.
Under the bludgeonings of chance
    My head is bloody, but unbowed.

Beyond this place of wrath and tears
    Looms but the horror of the shade,
And yet the menace of the years
    Finds, and shall find me, unafraid.

It matters not how strait the gate,
    How charged with punishments the scroll,
I am the master of my fate;
    I am the captain of my soul.

The Pulley

GEORGE HERBERT

When God at first made Man,
Having a glass of blessings standing by—
Let us (said He) pour on him all we can;
Let the world's riches, which dispersèd lie,
    Contract into a span.

So strength first made a way,
Then beauty flowed, then wisdom, honor, pleasure:
When almost all was out, God made a stay,
Perceiving that, alone of all His treasure,
   Rest in the bottom lay.

   For if I should (said He)
Bestow this jewel also on My creature,
He would adore My gifts instead of Me,
And rest in Nature, not the God of Nature:
   So both should losers be.

   Yet let him keep the rest,
But keep them with repining restlessness;
Let him be rich and weary, that at least,
If goodness lead him not, yet weariness
   May toss him to My breast.

Time, You Old Gypsy Man

RALPH HODGSON

Time, you old gypsy man,
   Will you not stay,
Put up your caravan
   Just for one day?

All things I'll give you
Will you be my guest,
Bells for your jennet
Of silver the best,
Goldsmiths shall beat you
A great golden ring,
Peacocks shall bow to you,
Little boys sing,

Oh, and sweet girls will
Festoon you with may.
Time, you old gypsy,
Why hasten away?

Last week in Babylon,
Last night in Rome,
Morning, and in the crush
Under Paul's dome;
Under Paul's dial
You tighten your rein—
Only a moment,
And off once again;
Off to some city
Now blind in the womb,
Off to another
Ere that's in the tomb.

Time, you old gypsy man,
    Will you not stay,
Put up your caravan
    Just for one day?

Gradatim

JOSIAH GILBERT HOLLAND

Heaven is not gained at a single bound;
    But we build the ladder by which we rise
    From the lowly earth to the vaulted skies,
And we mount to its summit round by round.

I count this thing to be grandly true,
    That a noble deed is a step toward God—
    Lifting the soul from the common sod
To a purer air and a broader view.

We rise by things that are 'neath our feet;
    By what we have mastered of good and gain;
    By the pride deposed and the passion slain,
And the vanquished ills that we hourly meet.

We hope, we aspire, we resolve, we trust,
    When the morning calls us to life and light,
    But our hearts grow weary, and, ere the night,
Our lives are trailing the sordid dust.

We hope, we resolve, we aspire, we pray,
    And we think that we mount the air on wings
    Beyond the recall of sensual things,
While our feet still cling to the heavy clay.

Wings for the angels, but feet for men!
    We may borrow the wings to find the way—
    We may hope, and resolve, and aspire, and pray,
But our feet must rise, or we fall again.

Only in dreams is a ladder thrown
    From the weary earth to the sapphire walls;
    But the dream departs, and the vision falls,
And the sleeper wakes on his pillow of stone.

Heaven is not reached at a single bound:
    But we build the ladder by which we rise
    From the lowly earth to the vaulted skies,
And we mount to its summit round by round.

The Chambered Nautilus

OLIVER WENDELL HOLMES

This is the ship of pearl which, poets feign,
   Sails the unshadowed main,—
   The venturous bark that flings
On the sweet summer wind its purpled wings
In gulfs enchanted, where the Siren sings,
   And coral reefs lie bare,
Where the cold sea-maids rise to sun their streaming hair.

Its webs of living gauze no more unfurl;
   Wrecked is the ship of pearl!
   And every chambered cell,
Where its dim dreaming life was wont to dwell,
As the frail tenant shaped his growing shell,
   Before thee lies revealed,—
Its irised ceiling rent, its sunless crypt unsealed!

Year after year beheld the silent toil
   That spread his lustrous coil;
   Still, as the spiral grew,
He left the past year's dwelling for the new,
Stole with soft step its shining archway through,
   Built up its idle door,
Stretched in his last-found home, and knew the old no
     more.

Thanks for the heavenly message brought by thee,
   Child of the wandering sea,
   Cast from her lap, forlorn!
From thy dead lips a clearer note is born
Than ever Triton blew from wreathèd horn!
   While on mine ear it rings,
Through the deep caves of thought I hear a voice that
     sings:—

Build thee more stately mansions, O my soul,
    As the swift seasons roll!
    Leave thy low-vaulted past!
Let each new temple, nobler than the last,
Shut thee from heaven with a dome more vast,
    Till thou at length art free,
Leaving thine outgrown shell by life's unresting sea!

God's Grandeur

GERARD MANLEY HOPKINS

The world is charged with the grandeur of God.
It will flame out, like shining from shook foil;
It gathers to a greatness, like the ooze of oil
Crushed. Why do men then now not reck his rod?

Generations have trod, have trod, have trod;
And all is seared with trade; bleared, smeared with toil;
And wears man's smudge and shares man's smell: the soil
Is bare now, nor can foot feel, being shod.

And for all this, nature is never spent;
There lives the dearest freshness deep down things;
And though the last lights off the black West went
Oh, morning, at the brown brink eastward, springs—
Because the Holy Ghost over the bent
World broods with warm breast and with ah! bright
    wings.

Pied Beauty

GERARD MANLEY HOPKINS

Glory be to God for dappled things—
    For skies of couple-colour as a brinded cow;
      For rose-moles all in stipple upon trout that swim;
Fresh-firecoal chestnut-falls; finches' wings;
    Landscape plotted and pieced—fold, fallow, and
      plough;
    And all trades, their gear and tackle and trim.
All things counter, original, spare, strange;
    Whatever is fickle, freckled (who knows how?)
      With swift, slow; sweet, sour; adazzle, dim;
He fathers-forth whose beauty is past change:
        Praise him.

Loveliest of Trees

A. E. HOUSMAN

Loveliest of trees, the cherry now
Is hung with bloom along the bough,
And stands about the woodland ride
Wearing white for Eastertide.

Now, of my threescore years and ten,
Twenty will not come again,
And take from seventy springs a score,
It only leaves me fifty more.

And since to look at things in bloom
Fifty springs are little room,
About the woodlands I will go
To see the cherry hung with snow.

The Sea Gipsy

RICHARD HOVEY

I am fevered with the sunset,
I am fretful with the bay,
For the wander-thirst is on me
And my soul is in Cathay.

There's a schooner in the offing,
With her topsails shot with fire,
And my heart has gone aboard her
For the Islands of Desire.

I must forth again to-morrow!
With the sunset I must be
Hull down on the trail of rapture
In the wonder of the Sea.

The Battle Hymn of the Republic

JULIA WARD HOWE

Mine eyes have seen the glory of the coming of the Lord:
He is trampling out the vintage where the grapes of wrath
are stored;
He hath loosed the fateful lightning of his terrible swift
sword:
His truth is marching on.

I have seen him in the watch-fires of a hundred circling
camps;
They have builded him an altar in the evening dews and
damps;
I can read his righteous sentence by the dim and flaring
lamps.
His day is marching on.

I have read a fiery gospel, writ in burnished rows of steel:
"As ye deal with my contemners, so with you my grace
    shall deal;
Let the Hero, born of woman, crush the serpent with his
    heel,
            Since God is marching on."

He has sounded forth the trumpet that shall never call
    retreat;
He is sifting out the hearts of men before his judgment-
    seat:
O, be swift, my soul, to answer him! be jubilant my feet!
            Our God is marching on.

In the beauty of the lilies Christ was born across the sea,
With a glory in his bosom that transfigures you and me;
As he died to make men holy, let us die to make men free,
            While God is marching on.

I, Too

LANGSTON HUGHES

I, too, sing America.

I am the darker brother.
They send me
to eat in the kitchen
When company comes,
But I laugh,
And eat well,
And grow strong.

Tomorrow,
I'll sit at the table
When company comes.

Nobody'll dare
Say to me,
"Eat in the kitchen,"
Then.

Besides,
They'll see
how beautiful I am
And be ashamed—

I, too, am America.

Abou Ben Adhem

LEIGH HUNT

Abou Ben Adhem (may his tribe increase!)
Awoke one night from a deep dream of peace,
And saw, within the moonlight in his room,
   Making it rich, and like a lily in bloom,
An Angel writing in a book of gold:
Exceeding peace had made Ben Adhem bold,
And to the Presence in the room he said,
"What writest thou?" The Vision raised its head,
And with a look made of all sweet accord
Answered, "The names of those who love the Lord."
"And is mine one?" said Abou. "Nay, not so,"
Replied the Angel. Abou spoke more low,
But cheerly still; and said, "I pray thee, then,
Write me as one that loves his fellow-men."

The Angel wrote, and vanished. The next night
It came again with a great wakening light,
And showed the names whom love of God had blessed,
And, lo! Ben Adhem's name led all the rest!

Jenny Kissed Me

LEIGH HUNT

Jenny kissed me when we met,
  Jumping from the chair she sat in;
Time, you thief, who love to get
  Sweets into your list, put that in!
Say I'm weary, say I'm sad,
  Say that health and wealth have missed me,
Say I'm growing old, but add,
    Jenny kissed me.

My City

JAMES WELDON JOHNSON

When I come down to sleep death's endless night,
The threshold of the unknown dark to cross,
What to me then will be the keenest loss,
When this bright world blurs on my fading sight?
Will it be that no more I shall see the trees
Or smell the flowers or hear the singing birds
Or watch the flashing streams or patient herds?
No. I am sure it will be none of these.

But, ah! Manhattan's sights and sounds, her smells,
Her crowds, her throbbing force, the thrill that comes
From being of her a part, her subtle spells,
Her shining towers, her avenues, her slums—
O God! the stark, unutterable pity,
To be dead, and never again behold my city.

To Celia

BEN JONSON

Drink to me only with thine eyes,
   And I will pledge with mine;
Or leave a kiss but in the cup
   And I'll not look for wine.
The thirst that from the soul doth rise
   Doth ask a drink divine;
But might I of Jove's nectar sup,
   I would not change for thine.

I sent thee late a rosy wreath,
   Not so much honouring thee
As giving it a hope that there
   It could not withered be;
But thou thereon didst only breathe
   And sent'st it back to me;
Since when it grows, and smells, I swear
   Not of itself, but thee!

On First Looking into Chapman's Homer

JOHN KEATS

Much have I travelled in the realms of gold,
And many goodly states and kingdoms seen;
Round many western islands have I been
Which bards in fealty to Apollo hold.
Oft of one wide expanse had I been told
That deep-browed Homer ruled as his demesne;
Yet did I never breathe its pure serene
Till I heard Chapman speak out loud and bold:
Then felt I like some watcher of the skies
When a new planet swims into his ken;

Or like stout Cortez when with eagle eyes
He stared at the Pacific—and all his men
Looked at each other with a wild surmise—
Silent, upon a peak in Darien.

Rouge Bouquet

JOYCE KILMER

In a wood they call the Rouge Bouquet
There is a new-made grave to-day,
Built by never a spade nor pick
Yet covered with earth ten metres thick.
There lie many fighting men,
    Dead in their youthful prime,
Never to laugh nor love again
    Nor taste the Summertime.
For Death came flying through the air
And stopped his flight at the dugout stair,
Touched his prey and left them there,
    Clay to clay.
He hid their bodies stealthily
In the soil of the land they fought to free
    And fled away.
Now over the grave abrupt and clear
    Three volleys ring;
And perhaps their brave young spirits hear
    The bugle sing:
"Go to sleep!
Slumber well where the shell screamed and fell.
Let your rifles rest on the muddy floor,
You will not need them any more.
Danger's past;
Now at last,
Go to sleep!"

There is on earth no worthier grave
To hold the bodies of the brave
Than this place of pain and pride
Where they nobly fought and nobly died.
Never fear but in the skies
    Saints and angels stand
Smiling with their holy eyes
    On this new-come band.
St. Michael's sword darts through the air
And touches the aureole on his hair
As he sees them stand saluting there,
    His stalwart sons:
And Patrick, Brigid, Columkill
Rejoice that in veins of warriors still
    The Gael's blood runs.
And up to Heaven's doorway floats,
    From the wood called Rouge Bouquet,
A delicate cloud of bugle notes
    That softly say:
"Farewell! Farewell.
Comrades true, born anew, peace to you!
Your souls shall be where the heroes are
And your memory shine like the morning-star.
Brave and dear,
Shield us here.
Farewell!"

If

RUDYARD KIPLING

If you can keep your head when all about you
    Are losing theirs and blaming it on you;
If you can trust yourself when all men doubt you,
    But make allowance for their doubting too:

If you can wait and not be tired by waiting,
  Or, being lied about, don't deal in lies,
Or being hated don't give way to hating,
  And yet don't look too good, nor talk too wise;

If you can dream—and not make dreams your master;
  If you can think—and not make thoughts your aim,
If you can meet with Triumph and Disaster
  And treat those two impostors just the same:
If you can bear to hear the truth you've spoken
  Twisted by knaves to make a trap for fools,
Or watch the things you gave your life to, broken,
  And stoop and build 'em up with worn-out tools;

If you can make one heap of all your winnings
  And risk it on one turn of pitch-and-toss,
And lose, and start again at your beginnings,
  And never breathe a word about your loss:
If you can force your heart and nerve and sinew
  To serve your turn long after they are gone,
And so hold on when there is nothing in you
  Except the Will which says to them: "Hold on!"

If you can talk with crowds and keep your virtue,
  Or walk with Kings—nor lose the common touch,
If neither foes nor loving friends can hurt you,
  If all men count with you, but none too much:
If you can fill the unforgiving minute
  With sixty seconds' worth of distance run,
Yours is the Earth and everything that's in it,
  And—which is more—you'll be a Man, my son!

On His Seventy-fifth Birthday

I strove with none; for none was worth my strife.
    Nature I loved, and next to Nature, Art;
I warmed both hands before the fire of life;
    It sinks, and I am ready to depart.

The New Colossus

EMMA LAZARUS

Not like the brazen giant of Greek fame,
With conquering limbs astride from land to land;
Here at our sea-washed, sunset gates shall stand
A mighty woman with a torch, whose flame
Is the imprisoned lightning, and her name
Mother of Exiles. From her beacon-hand
Glows world-wide welcome; her mild eyes command
The air-bridged harbor that twin cities frame.
"Keep, ancient lands, your storied pomp!" cries she
With silent lips. "Give me your tired, your poor,
Your huddled masses yearning to breathe free,
The wretched refuse of your teeming shore.
Send these, the homeless, tempest-tost to me.
I lift my lamp beside the golden door!"

The Spires of Oxford

WINIFRED M. LETTS

I saw the spires of Oxford
   As I was passing by,
The grey spires of Oxford
   Against a pearl-grey sky;
My heart was with the Oxford men
   Who went abroad to die.

The years go fast in Oxford,
   The golden years and gay;
The hoary colleges look down
   On careless boys at play,
But when the bugles sounded—War!
   They put their games away.

They left the peaceful river,
   The cricket field, the quad,
The shaven lawns of Oxford,
   To seek a bloody sod.
They gave their merry youth away
   For country and for God.

God rest you, happy gentlemen,
   Who laid your good lives down,
Who took the khaki and the gun
   Instead of cap and gown.
God bring you to a fairer place
   Then even Oxford town.

I Am an American

ELIAS LIEBERMAN

I am an American.
My father belongs to the Sons of the Revolution;
My mother, to the Colonial Dames.
One of my ancestors pitched tea overboard in Boston
     Harbor;
Another stood his ground with Warren;
Another hungered with Washington at Valley Forge.
My forefathers were America in the making:
They spoke in her council halls;
They died on her battle-fields;
They commanded her ships;
They cleared her forests.
Dawns reddened and paled.
Stanch hearts of mine beat fast at each new star
In the nation's flag.
Keen eyes of mine foresaw her greater glory:
The sweep of her seas.
The plenty of her plains.
The man-hives in her billion-wired cities.
Every drop of blood in me holds a heritage of patriotism.
I am proud of my past.
I AM AN AMERICAN.

I am an American.
My father was an atom of dust,
My mother a straw in the wind,
To His Serene Majesty.
One of my ancestors died in the mines of Siberia;
Another was crippled for life by twenty blows of the
     knout.
Another was killed defending his home during the
     massacres.

The history of my ancestors is a trail of blood
To the palace-gate of the Great White Czar.
But then the dream came—
The dream of America.
In the light of the Liberty torch
The atom of the dust became a man
And the straw in the wind became a woman
For the first time.
"See," said my father, pointing to the flag that fluttered
     near,
"That flag of stars and stripes is yours;
It is the emblem of the promised land.
It means, my son, the hope of humanity.
Live for it—die for it!"
Under the open sky of my new country I swore to do so;
And every drop of blood in me will keep that vow.
I am proud of my future.
I AM AN AMERICAN.

Abraham Lincoln Walks at Midnight

VACHEL LINDSAY

It is portentous, and a thing of state
That here at midnight, in our little town,
A mourning figure walks, and will not rest,
Near the old court-house pacing up and down,

Or by his homestead, or in shadowed yards
He lingers where his children used to play,
Or through the market, on the well-worn stones
He stalks until the dawn-stars burn away.

A bronzed lank man! His suit of ancient black,
A famous high top-hat and plain worn shawl
Make his the quaint great figure that men love,
The prairie-lawyer, master of us all.

He cannot sleep upon his hillside now.
He is among us:—as in times before!
And we who toss and lie awake for long
Breathe deep, and start, to see him pass the door.

His head is bowed. He thinks on men and kings.
Yea, when the sick world cries, how can he sleep?
Too many peasants fight, they know not why;
Too many homesteads in black terror weep.

The sins of all the war-lords burn his heart.
He sees the dreadnaughts scouring every main.
He carries on his shawl-wrapped shoulders now
The bitterness, the folly and the pain.

He cannot rest until a spirit-dawn
Shall come;—the shining hope of Europe free:
The league of sober folk, the Workers' Earth,
Bringing long peace to Cornland, Alp and Sea.

It breaks his heart that kings must murder still,
That all his hours of travail here for men
Seem yet in vain. And who will bring white peace
That he may sleep upon his hill again?

The Day Is Done

HENRY WADSWORTH LONGFELLOW

The day is done, and the darkness
   Falls from the wings of Night,
As a feather is wafted downward
   From an eagle in his flight.

I see the lights of the village
   Gleam through the rain and the mist,
And a feeling of sadness comes o'er me
   That my soul cannot resist:

A feeling of sadness and longing,
   That is not akin to pain,
And resembles sorrow only
   As the mist resembles the rain.

Come, read to me some poem,
   Some simple and heartfelt lay,
That shall soothe this restless feeling,
   And banish the thoughts of day.

Not from the grand old masters,
   Not from the bards sublime,
Whose distant footsteps echo
   Through the corridors of Time.

For, like strains of martial music,
   Their mighty thoughts suggest
Life's endless toil and endeavor;
   And tonight I long for rest.

Read from some humbler poet,
    Whose songs gushed from his heart,
As showers from the clouds of summer,
    Or tears from the eyelids start;

Who, through long days of labor,
    And nights devoid of ease,
Still heard in his soul the music
    Of wonderful melodies.

Such songs have power to quiet
    The restless pulse of care,
And come like the benediction
    That follows after prayer.

Then read from the treasured volume
    The poem of thy choice,
And lend to the rhyme of the poet
    The beauty of thy voice.

And the night shall be filled with music,
    And the cares, that infest the day,
Shall fold their tents, like the Arabs,
    And as silently steal away.

What Is So Rare as a Day in June?

JAMES RUSSELL LOWELL

No price is set on the lavish summer,
And June may be had by the poorest comer.
And what is so rare as a day in June?
    Then, if ever, come perfect days;
Then Heaven tries earth if it be in tune,
    And over it softly her warm ear lays:
Whether we look, or whether we listen,
We hear life murmur, or see it glisten;
Every clod feels a stir of might,
    An instinct within it that reaches and towers
And, groping blindly above it for light,
    Climbs to a soul in grass and flowers;
The flush of life may well be seen
    Thrilling back over hills and valleys;
The cowslip startles in meadows green,
    The buttercup catches the sun in its chalice,
And there's never a leaf or a blade too mean
    To be some happy creature's palace;
The little bird sits at his door in the sun,
    Atilt like a blossom among the leaves,
And lets his illumined being o'errun
    With the deluge of summer it receives;
His mate feels the eggs beneath her wings,
And the heart in her dumb breast flutters and sings;
He sings to the wide world, and she to her nest,—
In the nice ear of Nature which song is the best?

Horatius at the Bridge

THOMAS BABINGTON MACAULEY

Lars Porsena of Clusium,
　By the nine gods he swore
That the great house of Tarquin
　Should suffer wrong no more.
By the nine gods he swore it,
　And named a trysting-day,
And bade his messengers ride forth,
East and west and south and north,
　To summon his array.

East and west and south and north
　The messengers ride fast,
And tower and town and cottage
　Have heard the trumpet's blast.
Shame on the false Etruscan
　Who lingers in his home,
When Porsena of Clusium
　Is on the march for Rome.

The horsemen and the footmen
　Are pouring in amain
From many a stately market-place,
　From many a fruitful plain,
From many a lonely hamlet,
　Which, hid by beech and pine,
Like an eagle's nest, hangs on the crest
　Of purple Apennine;

From lordly Volaterrae,
　Where scowls the far-famed hold
Piled by the hands of giants
　For godlike kings of old;

From seagirt Populonia,
  Whose sentinels descry
Sardinia's snowy mountain-tops
  Fringing the southern sky;

From the proud mart of Pisae,
  Queen of the western waves,
Where ride Massilia's triremes
  Heavy with fair-haired slaves;
From where sweet Clanis wanders
  Through corn and vines and flowers,
From where Cortona lifts to heaven
  Her diadem of towers.

Tall are the oaks whose acorns
  Drop in dark Auser's rill;
Fat are the stags that champ the boughs
  Of the Ciminian hill;
Beyond all streams Clitumnus
  Is to the herdsman dear;
Best of all pools the fowler loves
  The great Volsinian mere.

But now no stroke of woodman
  Is heard by Auser's rill;
No hunter tracks the stag's green path
  Up Ciminian hill;
Unwatched along Clitumnus
  Grazes the milk-white steer;
Unharmed the water-fowl may dip
  In the Volsinian mere.

The harvests of Arretium,
  This year, old men shall reap;
This year, young boys in Umbro
  Shall plunge the struggling sheep;

And in the vats of Luna,
    This year, the must shall foam
Round the white feet of laughing girls
    Whose sires have marched to Rome.

There be thirty chosen prophets,
    The wisest of the land,
Who always by Lars Porsena
    Both morn and evening stand:
Evening and morn the Thirty
    Have turned the verses o'er,
Traced from the right on linen white
    By mighty seers of yore.

And with one voice the Thirty
    Have their glad answer given:
"Go forth, go forth, Lars Porsena,—
    Go forth, beloved of Heaven!
Go, and return in glory
    To Clusium's royal dome,
And hang round Nurscia's altars
    The golden shields of Rome."

And now hath every city
    Sent up her tale of men;
The foot are fourscore thousand,
    The horse are thousands ten.
Before the gates of Sutrium
    Is met the great array;
A proud man was Lars Porsena
    Upon the trysting-day.

For all the Etruscan armies
    Were ranged beneath his eye,
And many a banished Roman,
    And many a stout ally;

And with a mighty following,
    To join the muster, came
The Tusculan Mamilius,
    Prince of the Latian name.

But by the yellow Tiber
    Was tumult and affright:
From all the spacious champaign
    To Rome men took their flight.
A mile around the city,
    The throng stopped up the ways;
A fearful sight it was to see
    Through two long nights and days.

For aged folk on crutches,
    And women great with child,
And mothers, sobbing over babes
    That clung to them and smiled,
And sick men borne in litters
    High on the necks of slaves,
And troops of sunburnt husbandmen
    With reaping-hooks and staves.

And droves of mules and asses
    Laden with skins of wine,
And endless flocks of goats and sheep,
    And endless herds of kine,
And endless trains of wagons,
    That creaked beneath the weight
Of corn-sacks and of household goods,
    Choked every roaring gate.

Now, from the rock Tarpeian,
    Could the wan burghers spy
The line of blazing villages
    Red in the midnight sky.

The Fathers of the City,
    They sat all night and day,
For every hour some horseman came
    With tidings of dismay.

To eastward and to westward
    Have spread the Tuscan bands,
Nor house nor fence nor dovecote
    In Crustumerium stands.
Verbenna down to Ostia
    Hath wasted all the plain;
Astur hath stormed Janiculum,
    And the stout guards are slain.

I wis, in all the Senate,
    There was no heart so bold,
But sore it ached, and fast it beat,
    When that ill news was told.
Forthwith up rose the Consul,
    Up rose the Fathers all;
In haste they girded up their gowns,
    And hied them to the wall.

They held a council, standing
    Before the River-Gate;
Short time was there, ye well may guess,
    For musing or debate.
Out spake the Consul roundly:
    "The bridge must straight go down;
For, since Janiculum is lost,
    Naught else can save the town."

Just then a scout came flying,
    All wild with haste and fear:
"To arms! to arms! Sir Consul,—
    Lars Porsena is here."

On the low hills to westward
   The Consul fixed his eye,
And saw the swarthy storm of dust
   Rise fast along the sky.

And nearer fast and nearer
   Doth the red whirlwind come;
And louder still and still more loud,
From underneath that rolling cloud,
Is heard the trumpet's war-note proud,
   The trampling and the hum.
And plainly and more plainly
   Now through the gloom appears,
Far to left and far to right,
In broken gleams of dark-blue light,
The long array of helmets bright,
   The long array of spears.

And plainly, and more plainly,
   Above that glimmering line,
Now might ye see the banners
   Of twelve fair cities shine;
But the banner of proud Clusium
   Was highest of them all,—
The terror of the Umbrian,
   The terror of the Gaul.

And plainly and more plainly
   Now might the burghers know,
By port and vest, by horse and crest,
   Each warlike Lucumo:
There Cilnius of Arretium
   On his fleet roan was seen;
And Astur of the fourfold shield,
Girt with the brand none else may wield;
Tolumnius with the belt of gold;

And dark Verbenna from the hold
   By reedy Thrasymene.

Fast by the royal standard,
   O'erlooking all the war,
Lars Porsena of Clusium
   Sat in his ivory car.
By the right wheel rode Mamilius,
   Prince of the Latian name;
And by the left false Sextus,
   That wrought the deed of shame.

But when the face of Sextus
   Was seen among the foes,
A yell that rent the firmament
   From all the town arose.
On the house-tops was no woman
   But spat towards him and hissed,
No child but screamed out curses,
   And shook its little fist.

But the Consul's brow was sad,
   And the Consul's speech was low,
And darkly looked he at the wall,
   And darkly at the foe:
"Their van will be upon us
   Before the bridge goes down;
And if they once may win the bridge,
   What hope to save the town?"

Then out spake brave Horatius,
   The Captain of the Gate:
"To every man upon this earth
   Death cometh soon or late.
And how can man die better
   Than facing fearful odds

For the ashes of his fathers
 And the temples of his gods.

"And for the tender mother
 Who dandled him to rest,
And for the wife who nurses
 His baby at her breast,
And for the holy maidens
 Who feed the eternal flame,—
To save them from false Sextus
 That wrought the deed of shame?

"Hew down the bridge, Sir Consul,
 With all the speed ye may;
I, with two more to help me,
 Will hold the foe in play.
In yon strait path a thousand
 May well be stopped by three:
Now who will stand on either hand,
 And keep the bridge with me?"

Then out spake Spurius Lartius,—
 A Ramnian proud was he:
"Lo, I will stand at thy right hand,
 And keep the bridge with thee."
And out spake strong Herminius,—
 Of Titian blood was he:
"I will abide on thy left side,
 And keep the bridge with thee."

"Horatius," quoth the Consul,
 "As thou sayest, so let it be."
And straight against that great array
 Forth went the dauntless Three.
For Romans in Rome's quarrel
 Spared neither land nor gold,

Nor son nor wife, nor limb nor life,
    In the brave days of old.
.   .   .   .

Now while the Three were tightening
    Their harness on their backs,
The Consul was the foremost man
    To take in hand an axe:
And Fathers, mixed with Commons,
    Seized hatchet, bar, and crow,
And smote upon the planks above,
    And loosed the props below.

Meanwhile the Tuscan army,
    Right glorious to behold,
Came flashing back the noonday light,
Rank behind rank, like surges bright
    Of a broad sea of gold.
Four hundred trumpets sounded
    A peal of warlike glee,
As that great host with measured tread,
And spears advanced, and ensigns spread,
Rolled slowly towards the bridge's head,
    Where stood the dauntless Three.

The Three stood calm and silent,
    And looked upon the foes,
And a great shout of laughter
    From all the vanguard rose;
And forth three chiefs came spurring
    Before that deep array;
To earth they sprang, their swords they drew,
And lifted high their shields, and flew
    To win the narrow way:

Aunus, from green Tifernum,
    Lord of the Hill of Vines;

And Seius, whose eight hundred slaves
  Sicken in Ilva's mines;
And Picus, long to Clusium
  Vassal in peace and war,
Who led to fight his Umbrian powers
From that gray crag where, girt with towers,
The fortress of Nequinum lowers
  O'er the pale waves of Nar.

Stout Lartius hurled down Aunus
  Into the stream beneath;
Herminius struck at Seius;
  And clove him to the teeth;
At Picus brave Horatius
  Darted one fiery thrust,
And the proud Umbrian's gilded arms
  Clashed in the bloody dust.

Then Ocnus of Falerii
  Rushed on the Roman Three;
And Lausulus of Urgo,
  The rover of the sea;
And Aruns of Volsinium,
  Who slew the great wild boar,—
The great wild boar that had his den
Amidst the reeds of Cosa's fen,
And wasted fields, and slaughtered men,
  Along Albinia's shore.

Herminius smote down Aruns;
  Lartius laid Ocnus low;
Right to the heart of Lausulus
  Horatius sent a blow:
"Lie there," he cried, "fell pirate!
  No more, aghast and pale,
From Ostia's walls the crowd shall mark
The track of thy destroying bark;

No more Campania's hinds shall fly
To woods and caverns, when they spy
   Thy thrice accursèd sail!"

But now no sound of laughter
   Was heard among the foes;
A wild and wrathful clamor
   From all the vanguard rose.
Six spears' lengths from the entrance
   Halted that deep array,
And for a space no man came forth
To win the narrow way.

But, hark! the cry is Astur:
   And lo! the ranks divide;
And the great Lord of Luna
   Comes with his stately stride.
Upon his ample shoulders
   Clangs loud the fourfold shield,
And in his hand he shakes the brand
   Which none but he can wield.

He smiled on those bold Romans
   A smile serene and high;
He eyed the flinching Tuscans,
   And scorn was in his eye.
Quoth he, "The she-wolf's litter
   Stand savagely at bay;
But will ye dare to follow,
   If Astur clears the way?"

Then, whirling up his broadsword
   With both hands to the height,
He rushed against Horatius,
   And smote with all his might.
With shield and blade Horatius
   Right deftly turned the blow.

The blow, though turned, came yet too nigh;
It missed his helm, but gashed his thigh.
The Tuscans raised a joyful cry
  To see the red blood flow.

He reeled, and on Herminius
  He leaned one breathing-space,
Then, like a wild-cat mad with wounds,
  Sprang right at Astur's face.
Through teeth and skull and helmet
  So fierce a thrust he sped,
The good sword stood a handbreadth out
  Behind the Tuscan's head.

And the great Lord of Luna
  Fell at that deadly stroke,
As falls on Mount Alvernus
  A thunder-smitten oak.
Far o'er the crashing forest
  The giant arms lie spread;
And the pale augurs, muttering low,
  Gaze on the blasted head.

On Astur's throat Horatius
  Right firmly pressed his heel,
And thrice and four times tugged amain,
  Ere he wrenched out the steel.
"And see," he cried, "the welcome,
  Fair guests, that waits you here!
What noble Lucumo comes next
  To taste our Roman cheer?"

But at his haughty challenge
  A sullen murmur ran,
Mingled with wrath and shame and dread,
  Along that glittering van.

There lacked not men of prowess,
   Nor men of lordly race,
For all Etruria's noblest
   Were round the fatal place.

But all Etruria's noblest
   Felt their hearts sink to see
On the earth the bloody corpses,
   In the path the dauntless Three;
And from the ghastly entrance
   Where those bold Romans stood,
All shrank, like boys who, unaware,
Ranging the woods to start a hare,
Come to the mouth of the dark lair
Where, growling low, a fierce old bear
   Lies amidst bones and blood.

Was none who would be foremost
   To lead such dire attack:
But those behind cried "Forward!"
   And those before cried "Back!"
And backward now and forward
   Wavers the deep array;
And on the tossing sea of steel
To and fro the standards reel,
And the victorious trumpet-peal
   Dies fitfully away.

Yet one man for one moment
   Strode out before the crowd;
Well known was he to all the Three,
   And they gave him greeting loud:
"Now welcome, welcome, Sextus!
   Now welcome to thy home!
Why dost thou stay, and turn away?
   Here lies the road to Rome."

Thrice looked he at the city;
　　Thrice looked he at the dead;
And thrice came on in fury,
　　And thrice turned back in dread;
And, white with fear and hatred,
　　Scowled at the narrow way
Where, wallowing in a pool of blood,
　　The bravest Tuscans lay.

But meanwhile axe and lever
　　Have manfully been plied;
And now the bridge hangs tottering
　　Above the boiling tide.
"Come back, come back, Horatius!"
　　Loud cried the Fathers all.—
"Back, Lartius! back, Herminius!
　　Back, ere the ruin fall!"

Back darted Spurius Lartius;—
　　Herminius darted back;
And, as they passed, beneath their feet
　　They felt the timbers crack.
But when they turned their faces,
　　And on the farther shore
Saw brave Horatius stand alone,
　　They would have crossed once more;

But with a crash like thunder
　　Fell every loosened beam,
And, like a dam, the mighty wreck
　　Lay right athwart the stream:
And a long shout of triumph
　　Rose from the walls of Rome,
As to the highest turret-tops
　　Was splashed the yellow foam.

And, like a horse unbroken,
    When first he feels the rein,
The furious river struggled hard,
    And tossed his tawny mane,
And burst the curb, and bounded,
    Rejoicing to be free;
And whirling down, in fierce career
Battlement, and plank, and pier,
    Rushed headlong to the sea.

Alone stood brave Horatius,
    But constant still in mind,—
Thrice thirty thousand foes before,
    And the broad flood behind.
"Down with him!" cried false Sextus,
    With a smile on his pale face.
"Now yield thee," cried Lars Porsena,
    "Now yield thee to our grace."

Round turned he, as not deigning
    Those craven ranks to see;
Naught spake he to Lars Porsena,
    To Sextus naught spake he;
But he saw on Palatinus
    The white porch of his home;
And he spake to the noble river
    That rolls by the towers of Rome.

"O Tiber! Father Tiber!
    To whom the Romans pray,
A Roman's life, a Roman's arms,
    Take thou in charge this day!"
So he spake, and speaking, sheathed
    The good sword by his side,
And, with his harness on his back,
    Plunged headlong in the tide.

No sound of joy or sorrow
   Was heard from either bank;
But friends and foes in dumb surprise,
With parted lips and straining eyes,
   Stood gazing where he sank;
And when above the surges
   They saw his crest appear,
All Rome sent forth a rapturous cry,
And even the ranks of Tuscany
   Could scarce forbear to cheer.

But fiercely ran the current,
   Swollen high by months of rain:
And fast his blood was flowing,
   And he was sore in pain,
And heavy with his armor,
   And spent with clanging blows;
And oft they thought him sinking,
   But still again he rose.

Never, I ween, did swimmer,
   In such an evil case,
Struggle through such a raging flood
   Safe to the landing-place;
But his limbs were borne up bravely
   By the brave heart within,
And our good Father Tiber
   Bore bravely up his chin.

"Curse on him!" quoth false Sextus;—
   "Will not the villain drown?
But for this stay, ere close of day
   We should have sacked the town!"
"Heaven help him!" quoth Lars Porsena,
   "And bring him safe to shore;

For such a gallant feat of arms
    Was never seen before."

And now he feels the bottom;
    Now on dry earth he stands;
Now round him throng the Fathers
    To press his gory hands;
And now, with shouts and clapping,
    And noise of weeping loud,
He enters through the River-Gate,
    Borne by the joyous crowd.

They gave him of the corn-land,
    That was of public right,
As much as two strong oxen
    Could plough from morn till night;
And they made a molten image,
    And set it up on high,
And there it stands unto this day
    To witness if I lie.

It stands in the Comitium,
    Plain for all folk to see,—
Horatius in his harness,
    Halting upon one knee;
And underneath is written,
    In letters all of gold,
How valiantly he kept the bridge
    In the brave days of old.

And still his name sounds stirring
    Unto the men of Rome,
As the trumpet-blast that cries to them
    To charge the Volscian home;
And wives still pray to Juno

For boys with hearts as bold
As his who kept the bridge so well
    In the brave days of old.

And in the nights of winter
    When the cold north-winds blow,
And the long howling of the wolves
    Is heard amidst the snow;
When round the lonely cottage
    Roars loud the tempest's din,
And the good logs of Algidus
    Roar louder yet within;

When the oldest cask is opened,
    And the largest lamp is lit;
When the chestnuts glow in the embers,
    And the kid turns on the spit;
When young and old in circle
    Around the firebrands close;
When the girls are weaving baskets,
    And the lads are shaping bows;

When the goodman mends his armor,
    And trims his helmet's plume;
When the goodwife's shuttle merrily
    Goes flashing through the loom;
With weeping and with laughter
    Still is the story told,
How well Horatius kept the bridge
    In the brave days of old.

In Flanders Fields

JOHN MCCRAE

In Flanders fields the poppies blow
Between the crosses, row on row,
   That mark our place; and in the sky
   The larks, still bravely singing, fly
Scarce heard amid the guns below.

We are the Dead. Short days ago
We lived, felt dawn, saw sunset glow,
   Loved and were loved, and now we lie
     In Flanders fields.

Take up our quarrel with the foe:
To you from failing hands we throw
   The torch; be yours to hold it high.
   If ye break faith with us who die
We shall not sleep, though poppies grow
     In Flanders fields.

Recipe for a Marriage

PHYLLIS MCGINLEY
With a Curtsy to Mr. Burns

John Anderson my jo, John,
   When we were first acquaint,
I had a fault or so, John,
   And you were less than saint.
But once we'd said a brave "I do"
   And paid the parson's fee,
I set about reforming you
   And you reforming me.

John Anderson my jo, John,
    Our years have journeyed fair;
I think, as couples go, John,
    We've made a pleasant pair.
For us, contented man and wife,
    The marriage bond endures,
Since you have changed my way of life
    And I have altered yours.

Let captious people say, John,
    There's poison in that cup.
We found a simple way, John,
    To clear each difference up.
We could not swap our virtues, John,
    So this was our design:
All your bad habits I took on,
    While you adopted mine.
Until the final lightnings strike,
    It's comfortable to know
Our faults we share and share alike,
    John Anderson my jo.

Sea Fever

JOHN MASEFIELD

I must go down to the seas again, to the lonely sea and
    the sky,
And all I ask is a tall ship and a star to steer her by;
And the wheel's kick and the wind's song and the white
    sail's shaking,
And a gray mist on the sea's face, and a grey dawn
    breaking.

I must go down to the seas again, for the call of the
    running tide

Is a wild call and a clear call that may not be denied;
And all I ask is a windy day with the white clouds flying,
And the flung spray and the blown spume, and the sea-
    gulls crying.

I must go down to the seas again, to the vagrant gypsy life,
To the gull's way and the whale's way where the wind's
    like a whetted knife;
And all I ask is a merry yarn from a laughing fellow-rover,
And quiet sleep and a sweet dream when the long trick's
    over.

Renascence

EDNA ST. VINCENT MILLAY

All I could see from where I stood
Was three long mountains and a wood;
I turned and looked another way,
And saw three islands in a bay.
So with my eyes I traced the line
Of the horizon, thin and fine,
Straight around till I was come
Back to where I'd started from;
And all I saw from where I stood
Was three long mountains and a wood.
Over these things I could not see;
These were the things that bounded me;
And I could touch them with my hand,
Almost, I thought, from where I stand.
And all at once things seemed so small
My breath came short, and scarce at all.
But, sure, the sky is big, I said;
Miles and miles above my head;
So here upon my back I'll lie
And look my fill into the sky.

And so I looked, and, after all,
The sky was not so very tall.
The sky, I said, must somewhere stop,
And—sure enough!—I see the top!
The sky, I thought, is not so grand;
I 'most could touch it with my hand!
And, reaching up my hand to try,
I screamed to feel it touch the sky.

I screamed, and—lo!—Infinity
Came down and settled over me;
Forced back my scream into my chest,
Bent back my arm upon my breast,
And, pressing of the Undefined
The definition on my mind,
Held up before my eyes a glass
Through which my shrinking sight did pass
Until it seemed I must behold
Immensity made manifold;
Whispered to me a word whose sound
Deafened the air for worlds around,
And brought unmuffled to my ears
The gossiping of friendly spheres,
The creaking of the tented sky,
The ticking of Eternity.

I saw and heard, and knew at last
The How and Why of all things, past,
And present, and forevermore.
The Universe, cleft to the core,
Lay open to my probing sense
That, sickening, I would fain pluck thence
But could not,—nay! But needs must suck
At the great wound, and could not pluck
My lips away till I had drawn
All venom out.—Ah, fearful pawn!

For my omniscience I paid toll
In infinite remorse of soul.
All sin was of my sinning, all
Atoning mine, and mine the gall
Of all regret. Mine was the weight
Of every brooded wrong, the hate
That stood behind each envious thrust,
Mine every greed, mine every lust.
And all the while for every grief,
Each suffering, I craved relief
With individual desire,—
Craved all in vain! And felt fierce fire
About a thousand people crawl;
Perished with each,—then mourned for all!
A man was starving in Capri;
He moved his eyes and looked at me;
I felt his gaze, I heard his moan,
And knew his hunger as my own.
I saw at sea a great fog-bank
Between two ships that struck and sank;
A thousand screams the heavens smote;
And every scream tore through my throat;
No hurt I did not feel, no death
That was not mine; mine each last breath
That, crying, met an answering cry
From the compassion that was I.
All suffering mine, and mine its rod;
Mine, pity like the pity of God.
Ah, awful weight! Infinity
Pressed down upon the finite me!
My anguished spirit, like a bird,
Beating against my lips I heard;
Yet lay the weight so close about
There was no room for it without.
And so beneath the weight lay I
And suffered death, but could not die.

Long had I lain thus, craving death,
When quietly the earth beneath
Gave way, and inch by inch, so great
At last had grown the crushing weight,
Into the earth I sank till I
Full six feet under ground did lie,
And sank no more,—there is no weight
Can follow here, however great.
From off my breast I felt it roll,
And as it went my tortured soul
Burst forth and fled in such a gust
That all about me swirled the dust.

Deep in the earth I rested now;
Cool is its hand upon the brow
And soft its breast beneath the head
Of one who is so gladly dead.
And all at once, and over all
The pitying rain began to fall;
I lay and heard each pattering hoof
Upon my lowly, thatched roof,
And seemed to love the sound far more
Than ever I had done before.
For rain it hath a friendly sound
To one who's six feet under ground;
And scarce the friendly voice or face:
A grave is such a quiet place.

The rain, I said, is kind to come
And speak to me in my new home.
I would I were alive again
To kiss the fingers of the rain,
To drink into my eyes the shine
Of every slanting silver line,
To catch the freshened, fragrant breeze
From drenched and dripping apple-trees.

For soon the shower will be done,
And then the broad face of the sun
Will laugh above the rain-soaked earth
Until the world with answering mirth
Shakes joyously, and each round drop
Rolls, twinkling, from its grass-blade top.
How can I bear it; buried here,
While overhead the sky grows clear
And blue again after the storm?
O, multi-colored, multiform,
Beloved beauty over me,
That I shall never, never see
Again! Spring-silver, autumn-gold,
That I shall never more behold!
Sleeping your myriad magics through,
Close-sepulchred away from you!
O God, I cried, give me new birth,
And put me back upon the earth!
Upset each cloud's gigantic gourd
And let the heavy rain, down-poured
In one big torrent, set me free,
Washing my grave away from me!

I ceased; and, through the breathless hush
That answered me, the far-off rush
Of herald wings came whispering
Like music down the vibrant string
Of my ascending prayer, and—crash!
Before the wild wind's whistling lash
That startled storm-clouds reared on high
And plunged in terror down the sky,
And the big rain in one black wave
Fell from the sky and struck my grave.

I know not how such things can be;
I only know there came to me

A fragrance such as never clings
To aught save happy living things;
A sound as of some joyous elf
Singing sweet songs to please himself,
And, through and over everything,
A sense of glad awakening.
The grass, a tip-toe at my ear,
Whispering to me I could hear;
I felt the rain's cool finger-tips
Brushed tenderly across my lips,
Laid gently on my sealed sight,
And all at once the heavy night
Fell from my eyes and I could see,—
A drenched and dripping apple-tree,
A last long line of silver rain,
A sky grown clear and blue again.
And as I looked a quickening gust
Of wind blew up to me and thrust
Into my face a miracle
Of orchard breath, and with the smell,—
I know not how such things can be!—
I breathed my soul back into me.

Ah! Up then from the ground sprang I
And hailed the earth with such a cry
As is not heard save from a man
Who has been dead, and lives again.
About the trees my arms I wound;
Like one gone mad I hugged the ground;
I raised my quivering arms on high;
I laughed and laughed into the sky,
Till at my throat a strangling sob
Caught fiercely, and a great heart-throb
Sent instant tears into my eyes;
O God, I cried, no dark disguise
Can e'er hereafter hide from me
Thy radiant identity!

Thou canst not move across the grass
But my quick eyes will see Thee pass,
Nor speak, however silently,
But my hushed voice will answer Thee.
I know the path that tells Thy way
Through the cool eve of every day;
God, I can push the grass apart
And lay my finger on Thy heart!

The world stands out on either side
No wider than the heart is wide;
Above the world is stretched the sky,—
No higher than the soul is high.
The heart can push the sea and land
Farther away on either hand;
The soul can split the sky in two,
And let the face of God shine through.
But East and West will pinch the heart
That can not keep them pushed apart;
And he whose soul is flat—the sky
Will cave in on him by and by.

Song in Exile

ALICE DUER MILLER

The rustling palms bend readily
    Between the sun and me;
The trades blow warm and steadily
    Across the turquoise sea;
But I'd rather feel the March wind bite
    In the country of the free.

Hibiscus and camellias
  Bloom here abundantly,
And roses and gardenias—
  The sweetest flowers there be—
But I'd rather see through the bare north woods
  One bridal dogwood tree.

The tropic light is mellow
  As a lamp in a lighted room;
The sun shines high and yellow
  In the quivering cloudless dome;
But, oh, for the snow and the cruel cold
  And the rigors of my home!

Columbus

JOAQUIN MILLER

Behind him lay the grey Azores,
  Behind the Gates of Hercules;
Before him not the ghost of shores,
  Before him only shoreless seas.
The good mate said: "Now must we pray,
  For lo! the very stars are gone.
Brave Admiral, speak, what shall I say?"
  "Why, say 'Sail on! sail on! and on!'"

"My men grow mutinous day by day;
  My men grow ghastly wan and weak."
The stout mate thought of home; a spray
  Of salt wave washed his swarthy cheek.
"What shall I say, brave Admiral, say,
  If we sight naught but seas at dawn?"
"Why, you shall say at break of day,
  'Sail on! sail on! sail on! and on!'"

They sailed and sailed, as winds might blow,
    Until at last the blanched mate said,
"Why, now not even God would know
    Should I and all my men fall dead.
These very winds forget their way,
    For God from these dread seas is gone.
Now speak, brave Admiral, speak and say"—
    He said: "Sail on! sail on! and on!"

They sailed. They sailed. Then spake the mate:
    "This mad sea shows his teeth to-night.
He curls his lip, he lies in wait,
    With lifted teeth, as if to bite!
Brave Admiral, say but one good word:
    What shall we do when hope is gone?"
The words leapt like a leaping sword:
    "Sail on! sail on! sail on! and on!"

Then, pale and worn, he kept his deck,
    And peered through darkness. Ah, that night
Of all dark nights! And then a speck—
    A light! a light! a light! a light!
It grew, a starlit flag unfurled!
    It grew to be Time's burst of dawn.
He gained a world; he gave that world
    Its grandest lesson: "On! sail on!"

On His Blindness

JOHN MILTON

When I consider how my light is spent
Ere half my days in this dark world and wide,
And that one talent which is death to hide
Lodged with me useless, though my soul more bent

To serve therewith my Maker, and present
My true account, lest He returning chide,
"Doth God exact day-labour, light denied?"
I fondly ask. But Patience, to prevent
That murmur, soon replies, "God doth not need
Either man's work or his own gifts. Who best
Bear his mild yoke, they serve him best. His state
Is kingly: thousands at his bidding speed,
And post o'er land and ocean without rest;
They also serve who only stand and wait."

The Pillar of the Cloud

JOHN HENRY NEWMAN

Lead, Kindly Light, amid the encircling gloom,
    Lead Thou me on!
The night is dark, and I am far from home—
    Lead Thou me on!
Keep Thou my feet; I do not ask to see
The distant scene—one step enough for me.

I was not ever thus, nor pray'd that Thou
    Shouldst lead me on;
I loved to choose and see my path; but now
    Lead Thou me on!
I loved the garish day, and, spite of fears,
Pride ruled my will: remember not past years.

So long Thy power hath blest me, sure it still
    Will lead me on,
O'er moor and fen, o'er crag and torrent, till
    The night is gone,
And with the morn those angel faces smile
Which I have loved long since, and lost awhile.

The Highwayman

ALFRED NOYES

The wind was a torrent of darkness among the gusty trees,
The moon was a ghostly galleon tossed upon cloudy seas,
The road was a ribbon of moonlight over the purple moor,
And the highwayman came riding—
　　　Riding—riding—
The highwayman came riding, up to the old inn-door.

He'd a French cocked-hat on his forehead, a bunch of lace
　　at his chin,
A coat of the claret velvet, and breeches of brown doe-skin;
They fitted with never a wrinkle: his boots were up to the
　　thigh!
And he rode with a jeweled twinkle,
　　　His pistol butts a-twinkle,
His rapier hilt a-twinkle, under the jeweled sky.

Over the cobbles he clattered and clashed in the dark inn-
　　yard,
And he tapped with his whip on the shutters, but all was
　　locked and barred;
He whistled a tune to the window, and who should be
　　waiting there
But the landlord's black-eyed daughter,
　　　Bess, the landlord's daughter,
Plaiting a dark red love-knot into her long black hair.

And dark in the dark old inn-yard a stable-wicket creaked
Where Tim the ostler listened; his face was white and
　　peaked;
His eyes were hollows of madness, his hair like mouldy
　　hay,

But he loved the landlord's daughter,
     The landlord's red-lipped daughter,
Dumb as a dog he listened, and he heard the robber say—

"One kiss, my bonny sweetheart, I'm after a prize to-night,
But I shall be back with the yellow gold before the
    morning light;
Yet, if they press me sharply, and harry me through the
    day,
Then look for me by moonlight,
     Watch for me by moonlight,
I'll come to thee by moonlight, though hell should bar the
    way."

He rose upright in the stirrups; he scarce could reach her
    hand,
But she loosened her hair i' the casement! His face burnt
    like a brand
As the black cascade of perfume came tumbling over his
    breast;
And he kissed its waves in the moonlight,
     (Oh, sweet black waves in the moonlight!)
Then he tugged at his reins in the moonlight, and galloped
    away to the West.

He did not come in the dawning; he did not come at noon;
And out o' the tawny sunset, before the rise o' the moon,
When the road was a gipsy's ribbon, looping the purple
    moor,
A red-coat troop came marching—
     Marching—marching—
King George's men came marching, up to the old inn-door.

They said no word to the landlord, they drank his ale
    instead,
But they gagged his daughter and bound her to the foot of
    her narrow bed;

Two of them knelt at her casement, with muskets at their
    side!
There was death at every window;
        And hell at one dark window;
For Bess could see, through her casement, the road that *he*
    would ride.

They had tied her up to attention, with many a sniggering
    jest;
They had bound a musket beside her, with the barrel
    beneath her breast!
"Now keep good watch!" and they kissed her.
She heard the dead man say—
Look for me by moonlight;
        Watch for me by moonlight;
*I'll come to thee by moonlight, though hell should bar the
    way!*

She twisted her hands behind her; but all the knots held
    good!
She writhed her hands till her fingers were wet with sweat
    or blood!
They stretched and strained in the darkness, and the hours
    crawled by like years,
Till, now, on the stroke of midnight,
        Cold, on the stroke of midnight,
The tip of one finger touched it! The trigger at least was
    hers!

The tip of one finger touched it; she strove no more for the
    rest!
Up, she stood up to attention, with the barrel beneath her
    breast,
She would not risk their hearing; she would not strive
    again;

For the road lay bare in the moonlight;
        Blank and bare in the moonlight;
And the blood of her veins in the moonlight throbbed to
        her love's refrain.

Tlot-tlot; tlot-tlot! Had they heard it? The horse-hoofs
        ringing clear;
Tlot-tlot, tlot-tlot, in the distance? Were they deaf that
        they did not hear?
Down the ribbon of moonlight, over the brow of the hill,
The highwayman came riding,
        Riding, riding!
The red-coats looked to their priming! She stood up,
        straight and still!

Tlot-tlot, in the frosty silence! *Tlot-tlot,* in the echoing
        night!
Nearer he came and nearer! Her face was like a light!
Her eyes grew wide for a moment; she drew one last deep
        breath,
Then her finger moved in the moonlight,
        Her musket shattered the moonlight,
Shattered her breast in the moonlight and warned him—
        with her death.

He turned; he spurred to the West; he did not know who
        stood
Bowed, with her head o'er the musket, drenched with her
        own red blood!
Not till the dawn he heard it; his face grew grey to hear
How Bess, the landlord's daughter,
        The landlord's black-eyed daughter,
Had watched for her love in the moonlight, and died in
        the darkness there.

Back, he spurred like a madman, shrieking a curse to the
    sky,
With the white road smoking behind him and his rapier
    brandished high!
Blood-red were his spurs i' the golden noon; wine-red was
    his velvet coat,
When they shot him down on the highway,
        Down like a dog on the highway,
And he lay in his blood on the highway, with the bunch of
    lace at his throat.

And still of a winter's night, they say, when the wind is in
    the trees,
When the moon is a ghostly galleon tossed upon cloudy
    seas,
When the road is a ribbon of moonlight over the purple
    moor,
A highwayman comes riding—
        Riding—riding—
A highwayman comes riding, up to the old inn-door.

Over the cobbles he clatters and clangs in the dark inn-
    yard;
And he taps with his whip on the shutters, but all is
    locked and barred;
He whistles a tune to the window, and who should be
    waiting there
But the landlord's black-eyed daughter,
        Bess, the landlord's daughter,
Plaiting a dark red love-knot into her long black hair.

Ode

ARTHUR WILLIAM EDGAR O'SHAUGHNESSY

We are the music-makers,
   And we are the dreamers of dreams,
Wandering by lone sea-breakers,
   And sitting by desolate streams;
World-losers and world-forsakers,
   On whom the pale moon gleams:
Yet we are the movers and shakers
   Of the world forever, it seems.

With wonderful deathless ditties
We build up the world's great cities,
   And out of a fabulous story
   We fashion an empire's glory:
One man with a dream, at pleasure,
   Shall go forth and conquer a crown;
And three with a new song's measure
   Can trample a kingdom down.

We, in the ages lying
   In the buried past of the earth,
Built Nineveh with our sighing,
   And Babel itself with our mirth;
And o'erthrew them with prophesying
   To the old of the new world's worth;
For each age is a dream that is dying,
   Or one that is coming to birth.

The Ways

JOHN OXENHAM

To every man there openeth
A Way, and Ways, and a Way.
And the High Soul climbs the High Way,
And the Low Soul gropes the Low,
And in between, on the misty flats,
The rest drift to and fro.
But to every man there openeth
A High Way, and a Low;
And every man decideth
The Way his soul shall go.

The Toys

COVENTRY PATMORE

My little Son, who look'd from thoughtful eyes
And moved and spoke in quiet grown-up wise,
Having my law the seventh time disobey'd,
I struck him, and dismiss'd
With hard words and unkiss'd
—His Mother, who was patient, being dead.
Then, fearing lest his grief should hinder sleep,
I visited his bed,
But found him slumbering deep,
With darken'd eyelids, and their lashes yet
From his late sobbing wet.
And I, with moan,
Kissing away his tears, left others of my own;
For, on a table drawn beside his head,
He had put, within his reach,
A box of counters and a red-vein'd stone,
A piece of glass abraded by the beach.

And six or seven shells,
A bottle with bluebells,
And two French copper coins, ranged there with
    careful art,
To comfort his sad heart.
So when that night I pray'd
To God, I wept, and said:
Ah, when at last we lie with trancèd breath,
Not vexing Thee in death,
And Thou rememberest of what toys
We made our joys,
How weakly understood
Thy great commanded good,
Then, fatherly not less
Than I whom Thou hast moulded from the clay,
Thou'lt leave Thy wrath, and say,
"I will be sorry for their childishness."

Love Is Patient

SAINT PAUL

If I should speak with the tongues of men and angels
    but do not have love,
    I have become as sounding brass or a tinkling cymbal.
And if I have prophecy and know all mysteries
    and all knowledge
And if I have all faith so as to remove mountains,
    but do not have love, I am nothing.
And if I distribute all my goods to feed the poor,
    and if I deliver my body to be burned,
     yet do not have love, it profits me nothing.

Love is patient, is kind.
Love does not envy, is not pretentious,
   is not puffed up, is not provoked.
Love thinks no evil,
   does not rejoice over wickedness,
   but rejoices in the truth.
Love bears with all things, believes all things.
   hopes all things, endures all things.

Love never fails,
   whereas prophecies will disappear and
   tongues will cease,
   and knowledge will be destroyed.
For we know in part and we prophesy in part;
But when that which is perfect has come,
   that which was imperfect
   will be done away with.

When I was a child, I spoke as a child,
   I felt as a child, I thought as a child.
Now that I have become a man,
   I have put away the things of a child.

We see now through a mirror in an obscure manner,
   but then face to face.
Now I know in part,
   but then I shall know even as I have been known.
So there abide faith, hope and love,
   these three;
   but the greatest of these is love.

Sleep

CHARLES PÉGUY
Translated by Julian Green

I don't like the man who doesn't sleep, says God.
Sleep is the friend of man.
Sleep is the friend of God.
Sleep is perhaps the most beautiful thing I have created.
And I myself rested on the seventh day.
He whose heart is pure, sleeps. And he who sleeps has a
      pure heart.
That is the great secret of being as indefatigable as a child.
Of having that strength in the legs that a child has.
Those new legs, those new souls,
And to begin afresh every morning, ever new,
Like young hope, new hope.
But they tell me that there are men
Who work well and sleep badly.
Who don't sleep. What a lack of confidence in me.
It is almost more serious than if they worked badly and
      slept well.
Than if they did not work but slept, because laziness
Is not a greater sin than unrest,
It is not even so great a sin as unrest
And despair and lack of confidence in me.
I am not talking, says God, about those men
Who don't work and don't sleep.
Those men are sinners, to be sure. They have what they
      deserve.
Great sinners. It's their fault for not working.
I am talking about those who work and don't sleep.
I pity them. I am talking about those who work and who,
      in this,
Obey my commandment, poor children.

And who on the other hand lack courage, lack confidence,
    and don't sleep.
I pity them. I have it against them. A little. They won't
    trust me.
Like the child who innocently lies in his mother's arms,
    thus do they not lie
Innocently in the arms of my Providence.
They have the courage to work. They lack the courage to
    be idle.
They have enough virture to work. They haven't enough
    virtue to be idle.
To stretch out. To rest. To sleep.
Poor people, they don't know what is good.
They look after their business very well during the day.
But they haven't enough confidence in me to let me look
    after it during the night.
As if I wasn't capable of looking after it during one night.
He who doesn't sleep is unfaithful to Hope.
And it is the greatest infidelity.
Because it is infidelity to the greatest Faith.
Poor children, they conduct their business with wisdom
    during the day.
But when evening comes, they can't make up their minds,
They can't be resigned to trust my wisdom for the space of
    one night
With the conduct and the governing of their business.
As if I wasn't capable, if you please, of looking after it a
    little.
Of watching over it.
Of governing and conducting, and all that kind of stuff.
I have a great deal more business to look after, poor
    people,
I govern creation, maybe that is more difficult.
You might perhaps, and no harm done, leave your
    business in my hands, O wise men.

Maybe I am just as wise as you are.

You might perhaps leave it to me for the space of a night.

While you are asleep

At last

And the next morning you might find it not too badly
damaged perhaps.

The next morning it might not be any the worse perhaps.

I may yet be capable of attending to it a little. I am
talking of those who work

And who in this obey my commandment.

And don't sleep, and who in this

Refuse all that is good in my creation,

Sleep, all the good I have created,

And also refuse my commandment just the same.

Poor children, what ingratitude towards me

To refuse such a good

Such a beautiful commandment.

Poor children, they follow human wisdom.

Human wisdom says Don't put off until tomorrow

What can be done the very same day.

But I tell you that he who knows how to put off until
tomorrow

Is the most agreeable to God.

He who sleeps like a child

Is also he who sleeps like my darling Hope.

And I tell you Put off until tomorrow

Those worries and those troubles which are gnawing at
you today

And might very well devour you today.

Put off until tomorrow those sobs that choke you

When you see today's unhappiness.

Those sobs which rise up and strangle you.

Put off until tomorrow those tears which fill your eyes and
your head,

Flooding you, rolling down your cheeks, those tears which
stream down your cheeks.

Because between now and tomorrow, maybe I, God, will
    have passed by your way.
Human wisdom says: Woe to the man who puts off what
    he has to do until tomorrow.
And I say Blessed, blessed is the man who puts off what he
    has to do until tomorrow.
Blessed is he who puts off. That is to say Blessed is he who
    hopes. And who sleeps.

To Helen

EDGAR ALLAN POE

Helen, thy beauty is to me
Like those Nicéan barks of yore,
That gently, o'er a perfumed sea,
The weary, wayworn wanderer bore
To his own native shore.

On desperate seas long wont to roam,
Thy hyacinth hair, thy classic face,
Thy Naiad airs have brought me home
To the glory that was Greece,
And the grandeur that was Rome.

Lo! in yon brilliant window-niche
How statue-like I see thee stand,
The agate lamp within thy hand!
Ah, Psyche, from the regions which
Are Holy Land!

The Wonderful World

WILLIAM BRIGHTY RANDS

Great, wide, beautiful, wonderful World,
With the wonderful water round you curled,
And the wonderful grass upon your breast,
World, you are beautifully dressed.

The wonderful air is over me,
And the wonderful wind is shaking the tree—
It walks on the water, and whirls the mills,
And talks to itself on the top of the hills.

You friendly Earth, how far do you go,
With the wheat-fields that nod and the rivers that flow,
With cities and gardens and cliffs and isles,
And the people upon you for thousands of miles?

Ah! you are so great, and I am so small,
I hardly can think of you, World, at all;
And yet, when I said my prayers today,
A whisper inside me seemed to say,
"You are more than the Earth, though you are such a dot!
You can love and think, and the Earth cannot!"

"When the Frost Is on the Punkin"

JAMES WHITCOMB RILEY

When the frost is on the punkin and the fodder's in the
    shock
And you hear the kyouck and gobble of the struttin'
    turkey-cock,
And the clackin' of the guineys, and the cluckin' of the
    hens,

And the rooster's hallylooyer as he tiptoes on the fence;
O, it's then's the times a feller is a-feelin' at his best,
With the risin' sun to greet him from a night of peaceful
        rest,
As he leaves the house, bareheaded, and goes out to feed
        the stock,
When the frost is on the punkin and the fodder's in the
        shock.

They's something kindo' harty-like about the atmusfere
When the heat of summer's over and the coolin' fall is
        here—
Of course we miss the flowers, and the blossums on the
        trees,
And the mumble of the hummin'-birds and buzzin' of the
        bees;
But the air's so appetizin'; and the landscape through the
        haze
Of a crisp and sunny morning of the airly autumn days
Is a pictur' that no painter has the colorin' to mock—
When the frost is on the punkin and the fodder's in the
        shock.

The husky, rusty russel of the tossels of the corn,
And the raspin' of the tangled leaves, as golden as the
        morn;
The stubble in the furries—kindo' lonesome-like, but still
A-preachin' sermuns to us of the barns they growed to fill;
The strawstack in the medder, and the reaper in the shed;
The hosses in theyr stalls below—the clover overhead!—
O, it sets my hart a-clickin' like the tickin' of a clock,
When the frost is on the punkin and the fodder's in the
        shock!

Then your apples all is getherd, and the ones a feller
        keeps

Is poured around the celler-floor in red and yeller heaps;
And your cider-makin' 's over, and your wimmern-folk is
　　through
With their mince and apple-butter, and theyr souse and
　　saussage, too! . . .
I don't know how to tell it—but ef sich a thing could be
As the Angels wantin' boardin', and they'd call around
　　on *me*—
I'd want to 'comodate 'em—all the whole-indurin' flock—
When the frost is on the punkin and the fodder's in the
　　shock.

Flammonde

EDWARD ARLINGTON ROBINSON

The man Flammonde, from God knows where,
With firm address and foreign air,
With news of nations in his talk
And something royal in his walk,
With glint of iron in his eyes,
But never doubt, nor yet surprise,
Appeared, and stayed, and held his head
As one by kings accredited.

Erect, with his alert repose
About him, and about his clothes,
He pictured all tradition hears
Of what we owe to fifty years.
His cleansing heritage of taste
Paraded neither want nor waste;
And what he needed for his fee
To live, he borrowed graciously.

He never told us what he was,
Or what mischance, or other cause,
Had banished him from better days
To play the Prince of Castaways.
Meanwhile he played surpassing well
A part, for most, unplayable;
In fine, one pauses, half afraid
To say for certain that he played.

For that, one may as well forego
Conviction as to yes or no;
Nor can I say just how intense
Would then have been the difference
To several, who, having striven
In vain to get what he was given,
Would see the stranger taken on
By friends not easy to be won.

Moreover, many a malcontent
He soothed and found munificent;
His courtesy beguiled and foiled
Suspicion that his years were soiled;
His mien distinguished any crowd,
His credit strengthened when he bowed;
And women, young and old, were fond
Of looking at the man Flammonde.

There was a woman in our town
On whom the fashion was to frown;
But while our talk renewed the tinge
Of a long-faded scarlet fringe,
The man Flammonde saw none of that,
And what he saw we wondered at—
That none of us, in her distress,
Could hide or find our littleness.

There was a boy that all agreed
Had shut within him the rare seed
Of learning. We could understand,
But none of us could lift a hand.
The man Flammonde appraised the youth,
And told a few of us the truth;
And thereby, for a little gold
A flowered future was unrolled.

There were two citizens who fought
For years and years, and over nought;
They made life awkward for their friends,
And shortened their own dividends.
The man Flammonde said what was wrong
Should be made right; nor was it long
Before they were again in line,
And had each other in to dine.

And these I mention are but four
Of many out of many more.
So much for them. But what of him—
So firm in every look and limb?
What small satanic sort of kink
Was in his brain? What broken link
Withheld him from the destinies
That came so near to being his?

What was he, when we came to sift
His meaning, and to note the drift
Of incommunicable ways
That make us ponder while we praise?
Why was it that his charm revealed
Somehow the surface of a shield?
What was it that we never caught?
What was he, and what was he not?

How much it was of him we met
We cannot ever know; nor yet
Shall all he gave us quite atone
For what was his, and his alone;
Nor need we now, since he knew best,
Nourish an ethical unrest:
Rarely at once will nature give
The power to be Flammonde and live.

We cannot know how much we learn
From those who never will return,
Until a flash of unforeseen
Remembrance falls on what has been.
We've each a darkening hill to climb;
And this is why, from time to time
in Tilbury Town, we look beyond
Horizons for the man Flammonde.

Song

CHRISTINA GEORGINA ROSSETTI

When I am dead, my dearest,
    Sing no sad songs for me;
Plant thou no roses at my head,
    Nor shady cypress-tree:
Be the green grass above me
    With showers and dewdrops wet;
And if thou wilt, remember,
    And if thou wilt, forget.

I shall not see the shadows,
    I shall not feel the rain;
I shall not hear the nightingale
    Sing on, as if in pain:

And dreaming through the twilight
   That doth not rise nor set,
Haply I may remember,
   And haply may forget.

O World, Thou Choosest Not the Better Part

GEORGE SANTAYANA

O world, thou choosest not the better part!
It is not wisdom to be only wise,
And on the inward vision close the eyes,
But it is wisdom to believe the heart.
Columbus found a world, and had no chart,
Save one that faith deciphered in the skies;
To trust the soul's invincible surmise
Was all his science and his only art.
Our knowledge is a torch of smoky pine
That lights the pathway but one step ahead
Across a void of mystery and dread.
Bid, then, the tender light of faith to shine
By which alone the mortal heart is led
Unto the thinking of the thought divine.

"Scum o' the Earth"

ROBERT HAVEN SCHAUFFLER

At the gate of the West I stand,
On the island where nations throng.
We call them "scum o' the earth";

Stay, are we doing you wrong,
Young fellow from Socrates' land?—
You, like a Hermes lithe and strong
Fresh from the master Praxiteles' hand?
So you're of Spartan birth?
Descended, perhaps, from one of the band—
Deathless in story and song—
Who combed their long hair at Thermopylæ's pass? . . .
Ah, I forget what straits (alas!),
More tragic than theirs, more compassion-worth,
Have doomed you to march in our "immigrant class"
Where you're nothing but "scum o' the earth."

You Pole with the child on your knee,
What dower have you for the land of the free?
Hark! does she croon
The sad little tune
Chopin once mined from the Polish air
And mounted in gold for us to wear?
Now a ragged young fiddler answers
In wild Czech melody
That Dvořák took whole from the dancers.
And the heavy faces bloom
In the wonderful Slavic way;
The dull little eyes, the foreheads' gloom,
Are suddenly fair and gay.
While, watching these folk and their mystery,
I forget that we,
In our scornful mirth,
Brand them as "polacks"—and "scum o' the earth."

Genoese boy of the level brow,
Lad of the lustrous, dreamy eyes
Agaze at Manhattan's pinnacles now
In the first, glad shock of a hushed surprise;

Within your far-rapt seer's eyes
I catch the glow of the wild surmise
That played on the *Santa Maria*'s prow
In that still gray dawn,
Four centuries gone,
When a world from the wave began to rise.
Oh, who shall foretell what high emprise
Is the goal that gleams
When Italy's dreams
Spread wing and sweep into the skies?
Cæsar dreamed him a world ruled well;
Dante dreamed Heaven out of hell;
Angelo brought us there to dwell;
And you, are you of a different birth?—
You're only a "dago,"—and "scum o' the earth"!

Stay, are we doing you wrong
Calling you "scum o' the earth,"
Man of the sorrow-bowed head,
Of the features tender yet strong,—
Man of the eyes full of wisdom and mystery
Mingled with patience and dread?
Have not I known you in history,
Sorrow-bowed head?
Were you the poet-king, worth
Treasures of Ophir unpriced?
Or were you the prophet, whose art
Foretold how the rabble would mock
That shepherd of spirits, erelong,
Who should gather the lambs to his heart
And tenderly feed his flock?
Man—lift that sorrow-bowed head. . . .
Behold, the face of the Christ!

The vision dies at its birth.
You're merely a butt for our mirth.
You're a "sheeny"—and therefore despised
And rejected as "scum o' the earth."

Countrymen, bend and invoke
Mercy for us blasphemers,
For that we spat on these marvelous folk,
Nations of darers and dreamers,
Scions of singers and seers,
Our peers, and more than our peers.
"Rabble and refuse," we name them
And "scum o' the earth," to shame them.
Mercy for us of the few, young years,
Of the culture so callow and crude,
Of the hands so grasping and rude,
The lip so ready for sneers
At the sons of our ancient more-than-peers.
Mercy for us who dare despise
Men in whose loins our Homer lies;
Mothers of men who shall bring to us
The glory of Titian, the grandeur of Huss;
Children in whose frail arms may rest
Prophets and singers and saints of the West.

Newcomers all from the eastern seas,
Help us incarnate dreams like these.
Forgive and forget that we did you wrong.
Help us to father a nation strong
In the comradeship of an equal birth,
In the wealth of the richest bloods of earth.

I Waken to a Calling

DELMORE SCHWARTZ

I waken to a calling,
A calling from somewhere down, from a great height,
Calling out of pleasure and happiness,
And out of darkness, like a new light,
A delicate ascending voice,
Which seems forever rising, never falling
Telling all of us to rejoice,
To delight in the darkness and the light,
Commanding all consciousness forever to rejoice!

Lochinvar

SIR WALTER SCOTT

Oh! young Lochinvar is come out of the west,
Through all the wide Border his steed was the best;
And save his good broadsword he weapon had none,
He rode all unarmed and he rode all alone.
So faithful in love and so dauntless in war,
There never was knight like the young Lochinvar.

He stayed not for brake and he stopped not for stone,
He swam the Eske River where ford there was none;
But ere he alighted at Netherby gate,
The bride had consented, the gallant came late:
For a laggard in love and a dastard in war
Was to wed the fair Ellen of brave Lochinvar.

So boldly he entered the Netherby Hall,
Among bridesmen, and kinsmen, and brothers, and all:
Then spoke the bride's father, his hand on his sword,—
For the poor craven bridegroom said never a word,—

"Oh! come ye in peace here, or come ye in war,
Or to dance at our bridal, young Lord Lochinvar?"

"I long wooed your daughter, my suit you denied;
Love swells like the Solway, but ebbs like its tide—
And now am I come, with this lost love of mine,
To lead but one measure, drink one cup of wine.
There are maidens in Scotland more lovely by far,
That would gladly be bride to the young Lochinvar."

The bride kissed the goblet; the knight took it up,
He quaffed off the wine, and he threw down the cup.
She looked down to blush, and she looked up to sigh,
With a smile on her lips and a tear in her eye.
He took her soft hand ere her mother could bar,—
"Now tread we a measure!" said young Lochinvar.

So stately his form, and so lovely her face,
That never a hall such a galliard did grace;
While her mother did fret, and her father did fume,
And the bridegroom stood dangling his bonnet and plume;
And the bride-maidens whispered, " 'Twere better by far
To have matched our fair cousin with young Lochinvar."

One touch to her hand and one word in her ear,
When they reached the hall-door, and the charger stood
	near;
So light to the croupe the fair lady he swung,
So light to the saddle before her he sprung!
"She is won! we are gone, over bank, bush, and scaur;
They'll have fleet steeds that follow," quoth young
	Lochinvar.

There was mounting 'mong Graemes of the Netherby
	clan;
Forsters, Fenwicks, and Musgraves, they rode and they
	ran:

There was racing and chasing on Cannobie Lee
But the lost bride of Netherby ne'er did they see.
So daring in love and so dauntless in war,
Have ye e'er heard of gallant like young Lochinvar?

I Have a Rendezvous with Death

ALAN SEEGER

I have a rendezvous with Death
　At some disputed barricade
　When Spring comes round with rustling shade
And apple blossoms fill the air.
　I have a rendezvous with Death
When Spring brings back blue days and fair.

It may be he shall take my hand
And lead me into his dark land
　And close my eyes and quench my breath;
It may be I shall pass him still.
　I have a rendezvous with Death
On some scarred slope of battered hill,
　When Spring comes round again this year
　And the first meadow flowers appear.

God knows 'twere better to be deep
　Pillowed in silk and scented down,
Where love throbs out in blissful sleep,
　Pulse nigh to pulse, and breath to breath,
Where hushed awakenings are dear . . .
　But I've a rendezvous with Death
　　At midnight in some flaming town,
When Spring trips north again this year,
　And I to my pledged word am true,
　I shall not fail that rendezvous.

Fleurette

ROBERT W. SERVICE

My leg? It's off at the knee.
Do I miss it? Well, some. You see
I've had it since I was born;
And lately a devilish corn.
(I rather chuckle with glee
To think how I've fooled that corn.)

But I'll hobble around all right.
It isn't that, it's my face.
Oh, I know I'm a hideous sight,
Hardly a thing in place.
Sort of gargoyle, you'd say.
Nurse won't give me a glass,
But I see the folks as they pass
Shudder and turn away;
Turn away in distress . . .
Mirror enough, I guess.

I'm gay! You bet I *am* gay;
But I wasn't a while ago.
If you'd seen me even to-day,
The darndest picture of woe,
With this Caliban mug of mine,
So ravaged and raw and red,
Turned to the wall—in fine
Wishing that I was dead. . . .
What has happened since then,
Since I lay with my face to the wall,
The most despairing of men?
Listen! I'll tell you all.

That *poilu* across the way,
With the shrapnel wound on his head,

Has a sister; she came to-day
To sit a while by his bed.
All morning I heard him fret:
"Oh, when will she come, Fleurette?"

Then, sudden, a joyous cry;
The tripping of little feet;
The softest, tenderest sigh;
A voice so fresh and sweet;
Clear as a silver bell,
Fresh as the morning dews:
"C'est toi, c'est toi, Marcel!
Mon frère, comme je suis heureuse!"

So over the blanket's rim
I raised my terrible face,
And I saw—how I envied him!
A girl of such delicate grace;
Sixteen, all laughter and love;
As gay as a linnet, and yet
As tenderly sweet as a dove;
Half woman, half child—Fleurette.

Then I turned to the wall again.
(I was awfully blue, you see,)
And I thought with a bitter pain:
"Such visions are not for me."
So there like a log I lay,
All hidden, I thought, from view,
When sudden I heard her say:
"Ah! Who is that *malheureux?*"
Then briefly I heard him tell
(However he came to know)
How I'd smothered a bomb that fell
Into the trench, and so
None of my men were hit,
Though it busted me up a bit.

Well, I didn't quiver an eye,
And he chattered and there she sat;
And I fancied I heard her sigh—
But I wouldn't just swear to that.
And maybe she wasn't so bright,
Though she talked in a merry strain,
And I closed my eyes ever so tight,
Yet I saw her ever so plain:
Her dear little tilted nose,
Her delicate, dimpled chin,
Her mouth like a budding rose,
And the glistening pearls within;
Her eyes like the violet:
Such a rare little queen—Fleurette.

And at last when she rose to go,
The light was a little dim,
And I ventured to peep, and so
I saw her graceful and slim,
And she kissed him and kissed him, and oh
How I envied and envied him!
So when she was gone I said
In rather a dreary voice
To him of the opposite bed:
"Ah, friend, how you must rejoice!
But me, I'm a thing of dread.
For me nevermore the bliss,
The thrill of a woman's kiss."

Then I stopped, for lo! she was there,
And a great light shone in her eyes.
And me! I could only stare,
I was taken so by surprise,
When gently she bent her head:
"May I kiss you, sergeant?" she said.

Then she kissed my burning lips
With her mouth like a scented flower,
And I thrilled to the finger-tips,
And I hadn't even the power
To say: "God bless you, dear!"
And I felt such a precious tear
Fall on my withered cheek,
And, darn it, I couldn't speak.

And so she went sadly away,
And I know that my eyes were wet.
Ah, not to my dying day
Will I forget, forget!
Can you wonder now I am gay?
God bless her, that little Fleurette!

Sonnet XXIX

WILLIAM SHAKESPEARE

When, in disgrace with Fortune and men's eyes,
I all alone beweep my outcast state,
And trouble deaf heaven with my bootless cries,
And look upon myself, and curse my fate,
Wishing me like to one more rich in hope,
Featured like him, like him with friends possess'd
Desiring this man's art and that man's scope,
With what I most enjoy contented least;
Yet in these thoughts myself almost despising,
Haply I think on thee, and then my state,
Like to the lark at break of day arising
From sullen earth, sings hymns at heaven's gate;
    For thy sweet love remember'd such wealth brings
That then I scorn to change my state with kings.

All the World's a Stage

WILLIAM SHAKESPEARE

All the world's a stage,
And all the men and women merely players;
They have their exits and their entrances;
And one man in his time plays many parts,
His act being seven ages. At first, the infant,
Mewling and puking in the nurse's arms;
Then the whining school boy, with his satchel
And shining morning face, creeping like a snail
Unwillingly to school. And then the lover,
Sighing like a furnace, with a woeful ballad
Made to his mistress' eyebrow. Then a soldier,
Full of strange oaths and bearded like the pard,
Jealous in honour, sudden and quick in quarrel,
Seeking the bubble reputation
Even in the cannon's mouth. And then the justice,
In fair round belly with good capon lin'd,
With eyes severe and beard of formal cut,
Full of wise saws and modern instances;
And so he plays his part. The sixth age shifts
Into the lean and slipper'd pantaloon,
With spectacles on nose and pouch on side;
His youthful hose, well sav'd, a world too wide
For his shrunk shank; and his big manly voice,
Turning again toward childish treble, pipes
and whistles in his sound. Last scene of all,
That ends this strange eventful history
Is second childishness and mere oblivion;
Sans teeth, sans eyes, sans taste, sans everything.

                              AS YOU LIKE IT

Wolsey's Farewell to His Greatness

WILLIAM SHAKESPEARE

Farewell! a long farewell to all my greatness!
This is the state of man: to-day he puts forth
The tender leaves of hope; to-morrow blossoms,
And bears his blushing honours thick upon him;
The third day comes a frost, a killing frost,
And—when he thinks, good easy man, full surely
His greatness is a-ripening, nips his root,
And then he falls, as I do. I have ventured,
Like little wanton boys that swim on bladders,
This many summers in a sea of glory,
But far beyond my depth: my high-blown pride
At length broke under me, and now has left me,
Weary and old with service, to the mercy
Of a rude stream, that must for ever hide me.
Vain pomp and glory of this world, I hate ye!
I feel my heart new open'd. Oh, how wretched
Is that poor man that hangs on princes' favours!
There is, betwixt that smile we would aspire to,
That sweet aspect of princes, and their ruin,
More pangs and fears than wars or women have:
And when he falls, he falls like Lucifer,
Never to hope again.

HENRY VIII

Ozymandias

PERCY BYSSHE SHELLEY

I met a traveler from an antique land
Who said: Two vast and trunkless legs of stone
Stand in the desert. Near them, on the sand,
Half sunk, a shattered visage lies, whose frown,
And wrinkled lip, and sneer of cold command,
Tell that its sculptor well those passions read
Which yet survive, stamped on these lifeless things,
The hand that mocked them and the heart that fed;
And on the pedestal these words appear:
"My name is Ozymandias, king of kings:
Look on my works, ye Mighty, and despair!"
Nothing beside remains. Round the decay
Of that colossal wreck, boundless and bare,
The lone and level sands stretch far away.

The Fool's Prayer

EDWARD ROWLAND SILL

The royal feast was done; the King
   Sought some new sport to banish care,
And to his jester cried: "Sir Fool,
   Kneel now, and make for us a prayer!"

The jester doffed his cap and bells,
   And stood the mocking court before;
They could not see the bitter smile
   Behind the painted grin he wore.

He bowed his head, and bent his knee
   Upon the monarch's silken stool;

His pleading voice arose: "O Lord,
  Be merciful to me, a fool!

"No pity, Lord, could change the heart
  From red with wrong to white as wool,
The rod must heal the sin: but, Lord,
  Be merciful to me, a fool!

" 'Tis not by guilt the onward sweep
  Of truth and right, O Lord, we stay;
'Tis by our follies that so long
  We hold the earth from heaven away.

"These clumsy feet, still in the mire,
  Go crushing blossoms without end;
These hard, well-meaning hands we thrust
  Among the heart-strings of a friend.

"The ill-timed truth we might have kept—
  Who knows how sharp it pierced and stung?
The word we had not sense to say—
  Who knows how grandly it had rung?

"Our faults no tenderness should ask,
  The chastening stripes must cleanse them all;
But for our blunders—oh, in shame
  Before the eyes of heaven we fall.

"Earth bears no balsam for mistakes;
  Men crown the knave, and scourge the tool
That did his will; but Thou, O Lord,
  Be merciful to me, a fool!"

The room was hushed; in silence rose
  The King, and sought his gardens cool,
And walked apart, and murmured low,
  "Be merciful to me, a fool!"

The Battle of Blenheim

ROBERT SOUTHEY

It was a summer evening,
   Old Kaspar's work was done,
And he before his cottage door
   Was sitting in the sun,
And by him sported on the green
His little grandchild Wilhelmine.

She saw her brother Peterkin
   Roll something large and round,
Which he beside the rivulet
   In playing there had found;
He came to ask what he had found,
That was so large, and smooth, and round.

Old Kaspar took it from the boy,
   Who stood expectant by;
And then the old man shook his head,
   And with a natural sigh,
" 'Tis some poor fellow's skull," said he,
"Who fell in the great victory.

"I find them in the garden,
   For there's many hereabout;
And often when I go to plow,
   The plowshare turns them out!
For many thousand men," said he,
"Were slain in that great victory."

"Now tell me what 'twas all about,"
   Young Peterkin, he cries;
And little Wilhelmine looks up
   With wonder-waiting eyes;
"Now tell us all about the war,
And what they fought each other for."

"It was the English," Kaspar cried,
    "Who put the French to rout;
But what they fought each other for,
    I could not well make out;
But everybody said," quoth he,
"That 'twas a famous victory.

"My father lived at Blenheim then,
    Yon little stream hard by;
They burnt his dwelling to the ground,
    And he was forced to fly;
So with his wife and child he fled,
Nor had he where to rest his head.

"With fire and sword the country round
    Was wasted far and wide,
And many a childing mother then,
    And new-born baby died;
But things like that, you know, must be
At every famous victory.

"They say it was a shocking sight
    After the field was won;
For many thousand bodies here
    Lay rotting in the sun;
But things like that, you know, must be
After a famous victory.

"Great praise the Duke of Marlboro' won,
    And our good Prince Eugene."
"Why, 'twas a very wicked thing!"
    Said little Wilhelmine.
"Nay, nay, my little girl," quoth he,
"It was a famous victory.

"And everybody praised the Duke
    Who this great fight did win."

"But what good came of it at last?"
    Quoth little Peterkin.
"Why that I cannot tell," said he,
"But 'twas a famous victory."

I Think Continually of Those Who Were Truly Great

STEPHEN SPENDER

I think continually of those who were truly great.
Who, from the womb, remembered the soul's history
Through corridors of light where the hours are suns,
Endless and singing. Whose lovely ambition
Was that their lips, still touched with fire,
Should tell of the spirit clothed from head to foot in song.
And who hoarded from the spring branches
The desires falling across their bodies like blossoms.

What is precious is never to forget
The delight of the blood drawn from ageless springs
Breaking through rocks in worlds before our earth;
Never to deny its pleasure in the simple morning light,
Nor its grave evening demand for love;
Never to allow gradually the traffic to smother
With noise and fog the flowering of the spirit.

Near the snow, near the sun, in the highest fields
See how these names are fêted by the waving grass,
And by the streamers of white cloud,
And whispers of wind in the listening sky;
The names of those who in their lives fought for life,
Who wore at their hearts the fire's centre.
Born of the sun they traveled a short while towards the
    sun,
And left the vivid air signed with their honour.

J. F. K.

SISTER M. STANISLAUS, I.H.M.

The Shining Hour

It was high noon, the shining hour,
and there he stood:
magnificence and magnanimity
intrepidly assuming global agony.
Was this not greatness?

And is not greatness always
an inviolate willingness
to stand full height and free,
to shoulder agony?

The Giant

All of his life
he stood taller than
any around him.
And, when death poised
at the window
he could not see,
he sat taller than
all in the cavalcade,
so tall, the assassin
could make his mark,
certainly.

He died . . .
as he thought, as he willed,
as he walked,
GIANTLY!

The First Spring After

Who walks along Potomac banks
                        this spring
will savor loveliness. Yet will he
                        be aware
this spring is not the same:
flickers across the blossom-dowered
                        land
the shadow of a blue, eternal flame.

Requiem

ROBERT LOUIS STEVENSON

Under the wide and starry sky,
    Dig the grave and let me lie.
Glad did I live and gladly die.
    And I laid me down with a will.

This be the verse you grave for me:
Here he lies where he long'd to be;
Home is the sailor, home from sea,
    and the hunter home from the hill.

Barter

SARA TEASDALE

Life has loveliness to sell,
    All beautiful and splendid things,
Blue waves whitened on a cliff,
    Soaring fire that sways and sings,
And children's faces looking up,
Holding wonder like a cup.

Life has loveliness to sell,
    Music like a curve of gold,
Scent of pine trees in the rain,
    Eyes that love you, arms that hold,
And for your spirit's still delight,
Holy thoughts that star the night.

Spend all you have for loveliness,
    Buy it and never count the cost;
For one white singing hour of peace
    Count many a year of strife well lost,
And for a breath of ecstasy
Give all you have been, or could be.

Crossing the Bar

ALFRED TENNYSON

Sunset and evening star,
    And one clear call for me!
And may there be no moaning of the bar,
    When I put out to sea,

But such a tide as moving seems asleep,
    Too full for sound and foam,
When that which drew from out the boundless deep
    Turns again home.

Twilight and evening bell,
    And after that the dark!
And may there be no sadness of farewell,
    When I embark;

For tho' from out our bourne of Time and Place
    The flood may bear me far,
I hope to see my Pilot face to face
    When I have crossed the bar.

Casey at the Bat

ERNEST LAURENCE THAYER

It looked extremely rocky for the Mudville nine that
    day;
The score stood two to four, with but one inning left
    to play.
So, when Cooney died at Second, and Burrows did the
    same,
A pallor wreathed the features of the patrons of the
    game.

A straggling few got up to go, leaving there the rest,
With that hope which springs eternal within the human
    breast.
For they thought: "If only Casey could get a whack at
    that,"
They'd put even money now, with Casey at the bat.

But Flynn preceded Casey, and likewise so did Blake,
And the former was a pudd'n, and the latter was a fake.
So on that stricken multitude a deathlike silence sat;
For there seemed but little chance of Casey's getting
    to the bat.

But Flynn let drive a "single," to the wonderment of all,
And the much-despised Blakey "tore the cover off the
    ball."
And when the dust had lifted, and they saw what had
    occurred,
There was Blakey safe at second, and Flynn a-huggin'
    third.

Then from the gladdened multitude went up a joyous
    yell—
It rumbled in the mountaintops, it rattled in the dell;

It struck upon the hillside and rebounded on the flat;
For Casey, mighty Casey, was advancing to the bat.

There was ease in Casey's manner as he stepped into his
place,
There was pride in Casey's bearing and a smile on Casey's
face;
And when, responding to the cheers, he lightly doffed his
hat,
No stranger in the crowd could doubt 'twas Casey at the
bat.

Ten thousand eyes were on him as he rubbed his hands
with dirt;
Five thousand tongues applauded when he wiped them
on his shirt;
Then when the writhing pitcher ground the ball into his
hip,
Defiance glanced in Casey's eye, a sneer curled Casey's lip.

And now the leather-covered sphere came hurtling
through the air,
And Casey stood a-watching it in haughty grandeur there.
Close by the sturdy batsman the ball unheeded sped;
"That ain't my style," said Casey. "Strike one," the
umpire said.

From the benches, black with people, there went up a
muffled roar,
Like the beating of the storm-waves on a stern and distant
shore;
"Kill him! kill the umpire!" shouted some one on the stand;
And it's likely they'd have killed him had not Casey raised
his hand.

With a smile of Christian charity great Casey's visage
shone;

He stilled the rising tumult, he made the game go on;
He signaled to the pitcher, and once more the spheroid
    flew;
But Casey still ignored it, and the umpire said, "Strike
    two."

"Fraud!" cried the maddened thousands, and the echo
    answered "Fraud!"
But one scornful look from Casey and the audience was
    awed;
They saw his face grow stern and cold, they saw his
    muscles strain,
And they knew that Casey wouldn't let the ball go by
    again.

The sneer is gone from Casey's lips, his teeth are clenched
    in hate,
He pounds with cruel vengeance his bat upon the plate;
And now the pitcher holds the ball, and now he lets it go,
And now the air is shattered by the force of Casey's blow.

Oh, somewhere in this favored land the sun is shining
    bright,
The band is playing somewhere, and somewhere hearts
    are light;
And somewhere men are laughing, and somewhere
    children shout,
But there is no joy in Mudville—Mighty Casey has struck
    out.

Do Not Go Gentle
into That Good Night

DYLAN THOMAS

Do not go gentle into that good night,
Old age should burn and rave at close of day;
Rage, rage against the dying of the light.

Though wise men at their end know dark is right,
Because their words had forked no lightning they
Do not go gentle into that good night.

Good men, the last wave by, crying how bright
Their frail deeds might have danced in a green bay,
Rage, rage against the dying of the light.

Wild men who caught and sang the sun in flight,
And learn, too late, they grieved it on its way,
Do not go gentle into that good night.

Grave men, near death, who see with blinding sight
Blind eyes could blaze like meteors and be gay,
Rage, rage against the dying of the light.

And you, my father, there on the sad height,
Curse, bless, me now with your fierce tears, I pray.
Do not go gentle into that good night.
Rage, rage against the dying of the light.

The Hound of Heaven

FRANCIS THOMPSON

I fled Him, down the nights and down the days;
   I fled Him, down the arches of the years;
I fled Him, down the labyrinthine ways
   Of my own mind; and in the mist of tears
I hid from Him, and under running laughter.
          Up vistaed hopes I sped;
          And shot, precipitated,
   Adown Titanic glooms of chasmed fears,
From those strong Feet that followed, followed after.
         But with unhurrying chase,
         And unperturbéd pace,
     Deliberate speed, majestic instancy,
         They beat—and a Voice beat
         More instant than the Feet—
     "All things betray thee, who betrayest Me."
         I pleaded, outlaw-wise,
By many a hearted casement, curtained red,
   Trellised with intertwining charities;
(For, though I knew His love Who followéd,
         Yet was I sore adread
Lest, having Him, I must have naught beside);
But, if one little casement parted wide,
   The gust of His approach would clash it to.
Fear wist not to evade, as Love wist to pursue.
Across the margent of the world I fled,
     And troubled the gold gateways of the stars,
     Smiting for shelter on their clanged bars;
       Fretted to dulcet jars
And silvern clatter the pale ports o' the moon.
I said to Dawn: Be sudden—to Eve: Be soon;
     With thy young skiey blossoms heap me over
     From this tremendous Lover—
Float thy vague veil about me, lest He see!

I tempted all His servitors, but to find
My own betrayal in their constancy,
In faith to Him their fickleness to me,
      Their traitorous trueness, and their loyal deceit.
To all swift things for swiftness did I sue;
      Clung to the whistling mane of every wind.
         But whether they swept, smoothly fleet,
      The long savannahs of the blue;
            Or whether, Thunder-driven,
      They clanged his chariot 'thwart a heaven
Plashy with flying lightnings round the spurn o' their
      feet:—
      Fear wist not to evade as Love wist to pursue.
            Still with unhurrying chase,
            And unperturbéd pace,
      Deliberate speed, majestic instancy,
      Came on the following Feet,
            And a Voice above their beat—
      "Naught shelters thee, who wilt not shelter Me."

I sought no more that after which I strayed
      In face of man or maid;
But still within the little children's eyes
      Seems something, something that replies,
They at least are for me, surely for me!
I turned me to them very wistfully;
But just as their young eyes grew sudden fair
      With dawning answers there,
Their angel plucked them from me by the hair.
"Come then, ye other children, Nature's—share
With me" (said I) "your delicate fellowship;
            Let me greet you lip to lip,
            Let me twine with you caresses,
               Wantoning
            With our Lady-Mother's vagrant tresses,
               Banqueting

With her in her wind-walled palace,
Underneath her azured dais,
Quaffing, as your taintless way is,
    From a chalice
Lucent-weeping out of the dayspring,"
     So it was done:
I in their delicate fellowship was one—
Drew the bolt of Nature's secrecies.
I knew all the swift importings
    On the willful face of skies;
    I knew how the clouds arise
    Spumed of the wild sea-snortings;
    All that's born or dies
    Rose and drooped with; made them shapers
Of mine own moods, or wailful or divine;
    With them joyed and was bereaven.
    I was heavy with the even,
    When she lit her glimmering tapers
    Round the day's dead sanctities.
    I laughed in the morning's eyes.
I triumphed and I saddened with all weather,
    Heaven and I wept together,
And its sweet tears were salt with mortal mine.
Against the red throb of its sunset-heart
    I laid my own to beat,
    And share commingling heat;
But not by that, by that, was eased my human smart.
In vain my tears were wet on Heaven's grey cheek.
For ah! we know not what each other says,
    These things and I; in sound *I* speak—
Their sound is but their stir, they speak by silences.
Nature, poor stepdame, cannot slake my drouth;
    Let her, if she would owe me,
Drop yon blue bosom-veil of sky, and show me
    The breasts o' her tenderness:

Never did any milk of hers once bless
          My thirsting mouth.
          Nigh and nigh draws the chase,
          With unperturbéd pace,
     Deliberate speed, majestic instancy;
          And past those noiséd Feet
          A Voice comes yet more fleet—
     "Lo! naught contents thee, who content'st not Me."

Naked I wait Thy love's uplifted stroke!
My harness piece by piece Thou hast hewn from me,
          And smitten me to my knee;
          I am defenceless utterly.
          I slept, methinks, and woke,
And, slowly gazing, find me stripped in sleep.
In the rash lustihead of my young powers,
          I shook the pillaring hours
And pulled my life upon me; grimed with smears,
I stand amid the dust o' the mounded years—
My mangled youth lies dead beneath the heap.
My days have crackled and gone up in smoke,
Have puffed and burst as sun-starts on a stream.

          Yea, faileth now even dream
The dreamer, and the lute the lutanist;
Even the linked fantasies, in whose blossomy twist
I swung the earth a trinket at my wrist,
Are yielding; cords of all too weak account
For earth with heavy griefs so overplused.
          Ah! is Thy love indeed
A weed, albeit an amaranthine weed,
Suffering no flowers except its own to mount?
          Ah! must—
          Designer infinite!—
Ah! must Thou char the wood ere Thou canst limn with it?
My freshness spent its wavering shower i' the dust;

And now my heart is as a broken fount,
Wherein tear-drippings stagnate, spilt down ever
        From the dank thoughts that shiver
Upon the sighful branches of my mind.
        Such is; what is to be?
The pulp so bitter, how shall taste the rind?
I dimly guess what Time in mists confounds;
Yet ever and anon a trumpet sounds
From the hid battlements of Eternity;
Those shaken mists a space unsettle, then
Round the half-glimpsed turrets slowly wash again.
        But not ere him who summoneth
        I first have seen, enwound
With glooming robes purpureal, cypress-crowned;
His name I know, and what his trumpet saith.
Whether man's heart or life it be which yields
        Thee harvest, must Thy harvest-fields
        Be dunged with rotten death?

        Now of that long pursuit
        Comes on at hand the bruit;
        That Voice is round me like a bursting sea:
        "And is thy earth so marred,
        Shattered in shard on shard?
        Lo, all things fly thee, for thou fliest Me!
        Strange, piteous, futile thing!
Wherefore should any set thee love apart?
Seeing none but I makes much of naught?" (He said),
"And human love needs human meriting:
        How hast thou merited—
Of all man's clotted clay the dingiest clot?
        Alack, thou knowest not
How little worthy of any love thou art!
Whom wilt thou find to love ignoble thee,
        Save Me, save only Me?

» 147 «

All which I took from thee I did but take,
  Not for thy harms,
But just that thou might'st seek it in My arms.
  All which thy child's mistake
Fancies as lost, I have stored for thee at home:
  Rise, clasp My hand, and come!"

  Halts by me that footfall:
  Is my gloom, after all,
  Shade of His hand, outstretched caressingly?
"Ah, fondest, blindest, weakest,
  I am He Whom thou seekest!
  Thou dravest love from thee, who dravest Me."

Work

HENRY VAN DYKE

Let me but do my work from day to day,
  In field or forest, at the desk or loom,
  In roaring market-place or tranquil room;
Let me but find it in my heart to say,
When vagrant wishes beckon me astray,
  "This is my work; my blessing, not my doom;
  Of all who live, I am the one by whom
This work can best be done in the right way."
Then shall I see it not too great, nor small,
  To suit my spirit and to prove my powers;
  Then shall I cheerful greet the laboring hours,
And cheerful turn, when the long shadows fall,
At eventide, to play and love and rest,
Because I know for me my work is best.

I Hear America Singing

WALT WHITMAN

I hear America singing, the varied carols I hear,
Those of mechanics, each one singing his as it should be
    blithe and strong,
The carpenter singing his as he measures his plank or
    beam,
The mason singing his as he makes ready for work, or
    leaves off work,
The boatman singing what belongs to him in his boat, the
    deckhand singing on the steamboat deck,
The shoemaker singing as he sits on his bench, the hatter
    singing as he stands,
The wood-cutter's song, the ploughboy's on his way in the
    morning, or at noon intermission or at sundown,
The delicious singing of the mother, or of the young wife
    at work, or of the girl sewing or washing,
Each singing what belongs to him or her and to none else,
The day what belongs to the day—at night the party of
    young fellows, robust, friendly,
Singing with open mouths their strong melodious songs.

Maud Muller

JOHN GREENLEAF WHITTIER

Maud Muller on a summer's day
Raked the meadow sweet with hay.
Beneath her torn hat glowed the wealth
Of simple beauty and rustic health.
Singing, she wrought, and her merry glee
The mock-bird echoed from his tree.

But when she glanced to the far-off town,
White from its hill-slope looking down,
The sweet song died, and a vague unrest
And a nameless longing filled her breast;
A wish, that she hardly dared to own,
For something better than she had known.

The Judge rode slowly down the lane,
Smoothing his horse's chestnut mane:
He drew his bridle in the shade
Of the apple-trees, to greet the maid,
And asked a draught from the spring that flowed
Through the meadow across the road.

She stooped where the cool spring bubbled up,
And filled for him her small tin cup,
And blushed as she gave it, looking down
On her feet so bare, and her tattered gown.
"Thanks!" said the Judge; "a sweeter draught
From a fairer hand was never quaffed."

He spoke of the grass, and flowers, and trees,
Of the singing birds and the humming bees;
Then talked of the haying, and wondered whether
The cloud in the west would bring foul weather.
And Maud forgot her brier-torn gown,
And her graceful ankles bare and brown,
And listened, while a pleased surprise
Looked from her long-lashed hazel eyes.

At last, like one who for delay
Seeks a vain excuse, he rode away.
Maud Muller looked and sighed: "Ah me!
That I the Judge's bride might be!
He would dress me up in silks so fine,
And praise and toast me at his wine.

"My father should wear a broadcloth coat;
My brother should sail a painted boat;
I'd dress my mother so grand and gay,
And the baby should have a new toy each day;
And I'd feed the hungry and clothe the poor,
And all should bless me who left our door."

The Judge looked back as he climbed the hill,
And saw Maud Muller standing still.
"A form more fair, a face more sweet,
Ne'er has it been my lot to meet;
And her modest answer and graceful air
Show her wise and good as she is fair.

"Would she were mine, and I to-day,
Like her, a harvester of hay;
No doubtful balance of rights and wrongs,
Nor weary lawyers with endless tongues;
But low of cattle and song of birds,
And health, and quiet, and loving words."

But he thought of his sisters, proud and cold,
And his mother, vain of her rank and gold;
So, closing his heart, the Judge rode on,
And Maud was left in the field alone.
But the lawyers smiled that afternoon,
When he hummed in court an old love-tune;
And the young girl mused beside the well,
Till the rain on the unraked clover fell.

He wedded a wife of richest dower,
Who lived for fashion, as he for power.
Yet oft, in his marble hearth's bright glow,
He watched a picture come and go;
And sweet Maud Muller's hazel eyes,
Looked out in their innocent surprise.

Oft when the wine in his glass was red,
He longed for the wayside well instead;
And closed his eyes on his garnished rooms,
To dream of meadows and clover-blooms.
And the proud man sighed, with a secret pain,
"Ah, that I were free again!
Free as when I rode that day,
Where the barefoot maiden raked her hay."

She wedded a man unlearned and poor,
And many children played round her door;
But care and sorrow, and wasting pain,
Left their traces on heart and brain.
And oft when the summer sun shone hot
On the new-mown hay in the meadow lot,
And she heard the little spring brook fall
Over the roadside, through the wall,
In the shade of the apple-tree again
She saw a rider draw his rein,
And, gazing down with timid grace,
She felt his pleased eyes read her face.

Sometimes her narrow kitchen walls
Stretched away into stately halls;
The weary wheel to a spinnet turned;
The tallow candle and astral burned;
And for him who sat by the chimney lug,
Dozing and grumbling o'er pipe and mug,
A manly form at her side she saw,
And joy was duty and love was law.
Then she took up her burden of life again,
Saying only, "It might have been."

Alas for maiden, alas for Judge,
For rich repiner and household drudge!

God pity them both! and pity us all,
Who vainly the dreams of youth recall;
For of all sad words of tongue or pen
The saddest are these: "It might have been!"
Ah, well! for us all some sweet hope lies
Deeply buried from human eyes;
And in the hereafter angels may
Roll the stone from its grave away!

The Happy Warrior

WILLIAM WORDSWORTH

Who is the happy Warrior? Who is he
That every man in arms should wish to be?

It is the generous spirit, who, when brought
Among the tasks of real life, hath wrought
Upon the plan that pleased his boyish thought:
Whose high endeavors are an inward light
That makes the path before him always bright:
Who, with a natural instinct to discern
What knowledge can perform, is diligent to learn;
Abides by this resolve, and stops not there,
But makes his moral being his prime care;
Who, doomed to go in company with pain,
And fear, and bloodshed, miserable train!
Turns his necessity to glorious gain;
In face of these doth exercise a power
Which is our human nature's highest dower;
Controls them and subdues, transmutes, bereaves
Of their bad influence, and their good receives:
By objects, which might force the soul to abate
Her feeling, rendered more compassionate;

Is placable—because occasions rise
So often that demand such sacrifice;
More skilful in self-knowledge, even more pure,
As tempted more; more able to endure,
As more exposed to suffering and distress;
Thence also, more alive to tenderness.

'Tis he whose law is reason; who depends
Upon that law as on the best of friends;
Whence, in a state where men are tempted still
To evil for a guard against worse ill,
And what in quality or act is best
Doth seldom on a right foundation rest,
He labors good on good to fix, and owes
To virtue every triumph that he knows:
Who, if he rise to station of command,
Rises by open means; and there will stand
On honorable terms, or else retire,
And in himself possess his own desire;
Who comprehends his trust, and to the same
Keeps faithful with a singleness of aim;
And therefore does not stoop, nor lie in wait
For wealth, or honors, or for worldly state;
Whom they must follow; on whose head must fall,
Like showers of manna, if they come at all:
Whose power shed round him in the common strife,
Or mild concerns of ordinary life,
A constant influence, a peculiar grace;
But who, if he be called upon to face
Some awful moment to which Heaven has joined
Great issues, good or bad for human kind,
Is happy as a lover; and attired
With sudden brightness, like a man inspired;
And, through the heat of conflict, keeps the law
In calmness made, and sees what he foresaw;
Or if an unexpected call succeed,
Come when it will, is equal to the need:

He who, though thus endued as with a sense
And faculty for storm and turbulence,
Is yet a soul whose master-bias leans
To homefelt pleasures and to gentle scenes;
Sweet images! which, wheresoe'er he be,
Are at his heart; and such fidelity
It is his darling passion to approve;
More brave for this, that he hath much to love.
'Tis, finally, the Man, who, lifted high,
Conspicuous object in a Nation's eye,
Or left unthought-of in obscurity,—
Who, with a toward or untoward lot,
Prosperous or adverse, to his wish or not—
Plays, in the many games of life, that one
Where what he most doth value must be won
Whom neither shape of danger can dismay,
Nor thought of tender happiness betray;
Who, not content that former worth stand fast,
Looks forward, persevering to the last,
From well to better, daily self-surpassed:
Who, whether praise of him must walk the earth
For ever, and to noble deeds give birth,
Or he must fall, to sleep without his fame,
And leave a dead unprofitable name—
Finds comfort in himself and in his cause;
And, while the mortal mist is gathering, draws
His breath in confidence of Heaven's applause.

This is the happy Warrior; this is he
That every man in arms should wish to be.

The World Is Too Much with Us

WILLIAM WORDSWORTH

The world is too much with us; late and soon,
Getting and spending, we lay waste our powers:
Little we see in Nature that is ours;
We have given our hearts away, a sordid boon!
The Sea that bares her bosom to the moon;
The winds that will be howling at all hours,
And are up-gathered now like sleeping flowers;
For this, for everything, we are out of tune;
It moves us not.—Great God! I'd rather be
A Pagan suckled in a creed outworn;
So might I, standing on this pleasant lea,
Have glimpses that would make me less forlorn;
Have sight of Proteus rising from the sea;
Or hear old Triton blow his wreathèd horn.

When You Are Old

WILLIAM BUTLER YEATS

When you are old and grey and full of sleep,
And nodding by the fire, take down this book,
And slowly read, and dream of the soft look
Your eyes had once, and of their shadows deep;

How many loved your moments of glad grace,
And loved your beauty with love false or true;
But one man loved the pilgrim soul in you,
And loved the sorrows of your changing face;

And bending down beside the glowing bars,
Murmur, a little sadly, how Love fled
And paced upon the mountains overhead
And hid his face amid a crowd of stars.

Acknowledgments

For arrangements made with various authors and publishing houses where copyrighted material was permitted to be reprinted and for the courtesy extended by them, the following acknowledgments are gratefully made. All possible care has been taken to trace the ownership of every selection included and to make full acknowledgment for its use. If any errors have accidentally occurred, they will be corrected in subsequent editions, provided notification is sent to the publisher.

The American Press, for permission to use "The Geranium" by Leonard Feeney, S.J.

The American Tract Society, for permission to use "The Ways" by John Oxenham.

The Bobbs-Merrill Company, Inc., for permission to use "When the Frost Is on the Punkin" from *Joyful Poems for Children* by James Whitcomb Riley, copyright 1941, 1946, © 1960 by Lesley Payne, Elizabeth Eitel Miesse, and Edmund H. Eitel.

Jonathan Cape, Ltd., and Mrs. H. M. Davies, for permission to use "Leisure" from *The Complete Poems of W. H. Davies.*

J. M. Dent & Sons, Ltd., and the Trustees for the Copyrights of the late Dylan Thomas, for permission to use "Do Not Go Gentle into That Good Night" from *Collected Poems* by Dylan Thomas.

Dodd, Mead & Company, Inc., for permission to use "The Great Lover" from *The Collected Poems of Rupert Brooke,* copyright 1915 by Dodd, Mead & Company, Inc., copyright renewed 1943 by Edward Marsh; for permission to use

Index of First Lines

Author Index